DOMINIQUE'S
FRESH ⨳ FLAVORS

DOMINIQUE'S FRESH FLAVORS

Cooking with Latitude in New Orleans

Dominique Macquet
& John DeMers

TEN SPEED PRESS
Berkeley/Toronto

Ten Speed Press
Box 7123
Berkeley, California 94707
www.tenspeed.com
Distributed in Australia by Simon & Schuster Australia, in Canada by Ten Speed Press Canada, in New Zealand by Southern Publishers Group, in South Africa by Real Books, in Southeast Asia by Berkeley Books, and in the United Kingdom and Europe by Airlift Book Company.

The typographic scheme, case design, and jacket are by Jeff Puda.
Copyediting: Kristi Hein, Pictures and Words
Black and white photography: Sara Essex, New Orleans
Color photography: Becky Luigart-Stayner, Birmingham
Food styling: Fonda Shaia

Library of Congress Cataloging-in-Publication Data
Macquet, Dominique.
Dominique's fresh flavors : cooking with latitude in New Orleans / by Dominique Macquet and John DeMers.
p. cm.
ISBN 1-58008-153-3
1. Cookery, French. 2. Cookery — Louisiana — New Orleans. 3. Dominique's (Restaurant: New Orleans, La.) I. DeMers, John, 1952 – II. Title.
TX719.M214 2000
641.5944 — dc21
                                                                    00-055950

Printed in Canada
First printing, 2000
1 2 3 4 5 6 7 8 9 10 — 05 04 03 02 01 00

Acknowledgments

First and foremost, I'd like to thank my wife, Kendra, for inspiring me to write this book, typing all the recipes, and putting up with the hours of extra work. I wish to acknowledge my mom, Marie-Josee Macquet, who first got me interested in the pursuit of cooking, and also my mother-in-law, Carole LaNata, who provides me with her beautiful home-grown herbs.

Gratitude is also due to my staff at Dominique's for offering invaluable support during this project. Naturally, none of this could have begun without Thayer Lodging Group, namely Lee Pillsbury, who got me started, and Tom Kammerer and Peter Winters, who kept me going.

I extend a special thanks to pastry chef Ben Halstead for contributing his expertise in the desserts, as well as Megan Roen in New York, who tested the recipes. I also would like to thank those lending a welcome hand along the way: Farmer Lee Jones at Chef's Garden in Ohio, who kept me supplied with glorious organic produce; Gary Seafood in Florida, who filled my cookbook with the same gorgeous seafood that fills my restaurant's kitchen; and Pete Cappialli and Steven Garza at White Water Clams from whom I get my favorite baby conch.

Finally, a big thanks to Lorena Jones, Dennis Hayes, and all my friends at Ten Speed Press, who exercised enormous patience in guiding me through my first book and offered invaluable feedback, and finally in the end decided that, even more than seeing, tasting is believing.

Contents

The Latitude Attitude

*H*ere is your personal invitation to cook with latitude. It works in my restaurant's kitchen, and it will work in your kitchen too—filling your life not only with flavor but with fun. I hope you'll join me, by the time you've paged through this book, in believing this is quite an invitation.

I'm not, of course, asking you to come cook at Dominique's in New Orleans; that would be an immersion more intense than most diners have in mind. Then you'd be one more sous chef or pastry chef, swimming against the tide of restaurant life, trying to make culinary magic for 80 or 100 people—each of whom is the only guest that matters in his own mind. I'm sure I demand no less when I'm that diner, but it is a challenge no matter how you slice it. No, what I have in mind for you is something more pleasurable than getting a restaurant job: a liberation first of the mind and shortly thereafter of the spirit. Embrace those two liberations and the final liberation of your palate is sure to follow.

That's why Cooking with Latitude is the theme, the message of this book. So what does it mean to me, this notion of "cooking with latitude"? In some ways, the meaning is no more or less ambiguous than the word "latitude" itself. As most people know, latitude is a geographical term, meaning those invisible yet defining bands that ring our globe. There's no question that my life and career, beginning with my birth on the island of Mauritius in the Indian Ocean, has positioned me in the tropical latitudes. I've cooked many types of food in many types of climates, but the fact is that my culinary center remains tropical.

I love the lightness of tropical cuisines, from Southeast Asian to Caribbean, and I love the colorful, bursting-with-flavor ingredients that nature has been kind enough to let prosper in these areas. Most were originally introduced by man, but it was the tropical soil and climate that let them become what we know and love on the plate.

Secondly, the word latitude is about freedom to create, freedom from the chains and boxes within which all people (not just chefs) tend to live—the rules that dictate "It's done a certain way, therefore that's how it must be done." No one would claim there aren't good reasons for most classical techniques. But there are other ways to reach the same results—and best of all, there are other results!

My kitchen, I hope, is—even on the hard days—about having, claiming, taking, and giving the latitude in which great new ideas in food can happen.

Finally, there's the simple fact that "latitude" rhymes with "attitude," which Jimmy Buffet has employed in several of his tropical anthems. I don't, of course, mean bad attitude, the kind we mean when we say, "Hey, man, lose the attitude." As anyone who's ever cooked in a professional kitchen can attest, bad attitudes are more damaging than burners that won't light or sauces that break just when you need to serve them. There's just too much at stake for a bad attitude to be kept around.

No, in this case, I mean an attitude that reflects the tendencies of the tropical world as well as the wild impulse to create. It's got to be an attitude of openness and adventure, of letting people grow and explore. Sometimes in kitchens this feels a bit parental, as when you wisely allow your children to learn from actually making the same mistakes you made. But most often, it's not about parents but peers, people with whom you are very much in this together.

No matter who is leading, the voyage isn't always smooth and it isn't always fun. But on the best days, when you're "cooking with latitude," exploration and adventure are the unmarked destinations on the rumpled old treasure map each of us carries into the kitchen.

The Latitude Adventure

Some days, looking at a globe, it's a mystery to me how I ever made it off the island of Mauritius (MAW-reeshus). The place seems so far from the life I live now, a speck in the Indian Ocean off the eastern edge of Africa. Seen another way, there are few places I could be from that would strike my American diners as such a complete unknown. Africa sounds exotic, and most people can picture the dazzling blue waters, white sands, and towering palms of my oh-so-tropical birthplace. But if I asked my diners what I grew up eating, they'd have no clue.

That's because they don't know Mauritius (which the French call "Maurice," as in Chevalier). And that's because they don't know my mother.

Like many chefs I've met over the years, I spell my first culinary education with just three letters: MOM. I grew up in a household in which my bank-manager father did those important, mysterious things that paid the bills while my mother provided the peace and security in which my natural curiosity about taste could develop.

More than that, I was curious about taste because she was curious about taste. My adventure, taking me before I turned twenty farther than my mother had ever traveled, was in so many ways a kind of airline-ticket extension of hers.

You have to understand that while Mauritius is a long way from anywhere—certainly from my later life in London, Beverly Hills, and New Orleans—it carries an incredible slice of the world's diversity within its ring of white beaches. Mauritius is a melting pot, with strong French and British influences from the days of great empires, but also Indian, Chinese, and Arab populations from the immigrations that shaped parts of the Caribbean as well. Indeed, Mauritius is closer to the sources of these cultures than anyplace in the West.

The coasts and villages of islands such as mine became "lands of opportunity" for thousands over the centuries. These people spoke dozens of languages, worshiped according to hundreds of spiritual programs, and cooked with at least as many techniques, spices, and ambitions. It was my mother who took all these influences from the Mauritian melting pot and claimed them as the scents of home.

Wonderful curries were as natural to me as hamburgers or hot dogs would seem in America. They weren't foreign recipes, really—they were our mother's recipes. Stir-fries filling our house with the scents of ginger, garlic, and soy were not notions belonging to the Chinese people down the street, but natural expressions of my mother's kitchen. Ingredients for all these cuisines were available, since our island was convenient to the ancient spice trade—you remember, the one that built colonial empires in the first place. They were natural. Normal. Everyday. And for a long time, before I traveled to places blessed with no such excitement, I didn't know how lucky I was.

I don't remember ever wanting to work in my father's bank, though I might have when I was small. No, by the time I entered my teens I was dreaming of a career in hotels. The notion of food as commerce had already entered my mind, with a push from the baking my mother did for friends and clients in our own home kitchen. Wedding cakes (like the one she made for my wedding to

Kendra in New Orleans), special breads, party foods—all these were cooking in our house whenever family meals weren't. In fact, they were sometimes cooking at the same time. No wonder I figured I could work in a hotel!

That was the plan when at age sixteen I left Mauritius for hotel school in South Africa. And that was the goal when I wasn't giving my two years of "national service" expected of those living in that fast-changing country.

I apprenticed in a hotel in Durban, enjoying most my eye-opening work in the property's Japanese restaurant. Here was a cuisine my mother hadn't cooked, and I liked it so much I stayed an extra year. Japanese was a different way of looking at food, of understanding it, preparing it, and presenting it.

To build up my classical skills, I headed from South Africa to London, working in a French brasserie in Notting Hill Gate. Lo and behold, for all its classicism, the place had a New World thing going on too—not to mention a kitchen staff from Australia, New Zealand, Vietnam, and a lot of other countries whose food I'd never tasted. This job pointed me into my life's next adventure: cooking aboard a 150-foot sailing ship sent forth by Windstar to the Caribbean and French Polynesia.

This was hard work, breakfast, lunch, and dinner. But by now, you can guess what it meant to me: meeting new people, tasting new cuisines, staring at the towering peaks of places like Bora Bora, and knowing that the world is a big, diverse, intriguing place indeed.

Back in South Africa, I cooked more French in a restaurant called Tastevin in the Cape Sun Hotel, and also did time in the property's Italian eatery. By this point, though, politics was taking over the life of this beautiful country, with extremists on both sides causing trouble. I did have the honor, before leaving, of helping cook the first meal Nelson Mandela enjoyed after his release from prison. It seems he had a great meal.

It was now time, I was sure, to put my money where my mouth was—to explore and sample the cuisines that were beginning to appeal to me most. So I took off on an eight-month wander through Southeast Asia, doing a bit of observing at the old Raffles Hotel in Singapore but mostly just walking, talking, tasting. Through Malaysia and Burma I traveled, finally settling into the two places that changed everything I thought I knew about food.

The cuisines of Thailand and Vietnam made so much sense to me. They served up dish after dish that was light and fresh, with endless amounts of flavor, with no butter or cream. I was never a totally happy camper among the northern European classics; traveling on my stomach through Thailand and Vietnam sealed my fate forever.

The West did call me, however, or else I still might be there in that beautiful green jungle. It was my love of soccer (and my hero-worship of the team called Manchester City) that attracted me to that industrial city in northern England and convinced me to settle in at the Four Seasons Hotel. This was, ironically, one of the most classical places I ever worked, with gueridons rolled about the dining room and so many dishes finished tableside. I decided right then and there: If God had intended waiters to decide how a plate should look, there'd have been gueridons in the Garden of Eden!

Six months in Manchester gave way to another job in nearby Stockport, at a Michelin-starred restaurant called the White Cliff. And that gave way to a contract with Cunard, an agreement that took me around the world aboard the *Queen Elizabeth II*.

I think I wanted to build up my stamina, to prove to myself I could work incredibly hard. That I certainly did, laboring in the kitchen of the Queen's Grill from 6 to 10 A.M. for breakfast, noon to 3 P.M. for lunch, and 5:30 to 11 P.M. for dinner. Seven days a week. For four and a half months. In the kitchen, we joked that Cunard only did short contracts because they weren't sure who was going to survive.

With the *QEII* on my resume and my feet back in England to finish my contract, I found myself thinking more and more about one of the places we'd docked. In the middle of so many exotic ports, I recalled going ashore in one of the most exotic ports anywhere—the bizarre island known as Los Angeles.

I'd tasted my life's first "California cuisine" on Melrose Avenue. The meal was French at the same time it was Asian at the same time it was five or six other things. I was captured. That's what I wanted to eat, and that's what I wanted to cook. I longed for a cuisine that would constantly intrigue me. Knowing that I'd finally tasted it, I packed my bags and headed for LA.

Southern California proved formative for me, for its culinary freedom but also for its career opportunities. I served as sous chef at the Four Seasons in Beverly Hills, then at La Valencia Hotel in San Diego—then finally in my first executive chef's job (at age 28, doing California cuisine, no less) back in Beverly Hills at West Side Cafe. This work did many things for me. Most importantly, it pointed me toward New Orleans.

Not surprisingly, considering my life of travel, I knew next to nothing about the place that called me on the phone: the Bistro at the Hotel Maison de Ville in the French Quarter. But I was given a history that would slowly become so meaningful in my life.

The tiny place opened with a chef named Susan Spicer, who quickly made it a destination for diners from around the world. Susan had left, however, to open her own French Quarter restaurant called Bayona. After that, chefs had come and gone, up and down and all around, along with the Bistro's culinary mission and its reputation.

I was flown to New Orleans to cook for the people trying to find a new chef. I served them a six-course tasting of my strongest dishes. And I was offered the job.

You know, looking back, it's funny to think of all the different things I thought about New Orleans. It was no Beverly Hills,

I could tell. It was no California, with its wild leaping from fad to fad every other Tuesday. And at that time, New Orleans was no great farmer's market, so the fresh produce I'd come to demand was still only a fantasy here. But I loved the place anyway. I tried restaurant after restaurant, from the most traditional to the most creative. What I sensed then proved to be what I know now. The people of New Orleans are more serious about food than the people of Beverly Hills. Once you meet them where they are, once you share their love of how they live, they're excited to travel anywhere with you that you assure them they need to go.

As I say, I only figured that out later. But I understood it well enough, signing on at the Bistro, that I felt, somehow, I'd found a home.

During the nearly two years I cooked in that tiny kitchen, I'm proud of what went to the dining room. Before long—you can understand how much this meant to me—the Bistro became something more than "Susan Spicer's old place." We could, at last, think in the present tense, not just the past.

Reviews rolled in from national magazines, bringing the good fortune every chef hopes for. Guest chefs rolled in too, my favorite being the legendary Jean-Louis Palladin. In my kitchen that night, there was no question who the chef was—Jean-Louis.

It turns out, even when you are the chef, once in a while you have to step back and learn from the boss. Jean-Louis and I spent a marathon evening cooking a gala wine dinner together, then shot pool till almost dawn in some place I barely remember. In both disciplines, I'm sure my skills improved.

Eventually, the dream forming in the middle of all this hard work came true. It was a dream so shining that at times I couldn't even see it was there. But it was there. It was always there.

Just down the street from the Bistro, a successful hotel company named Thayer Lodging purchased the Maison Dupuy. And since for many years this property's restaurant could claim only to be "Paul Prudhomme's first New Orleans job," Thayer felt something dramatic had to be done. A statement had to be made. A signature restaurant had to be created. After the usual rounds of negotiation, we decided it was my signature that should propel this new restaurant into the new millennium.

During a dinner, I remember, Thayer president Lee Pillsbury asked about my plans for the future. All I could tell him was, "I'd like to have my own restaurant someday."

"Well," Mr. Pillsbury said, "how about next week?"

By the time the next week rolled around, I was in New York, picking out light fixtures, china, and silverware for what would indeed be my own restaurant.

Giving life to Dominique's has not been easy. We all know Murphy's Law, and I'm convinced Murphy must have had his inspiration working in a restaurant. Fine dining is such a production: a marriage of terrific cuisine, carefully chosen wines (a task I never tire of, sampling new vintages for our award-winning list), and staffing both the kitchen and the dining room. Through it all, you have to invite good people in. And through it all, you have to let good people out—going on to their next chapter, just as I've always done.

At the end of the night, when you're the chef, sometimes you're still the last one in the place. Surrounded by your reviews and your honors, you still have to know that, in some mysterious way, what you gave people on a plate that night to broaden their vision matters more than anything else.

It's a strange business, this cooking for a living. Unlike other arts that produce books or paintings or symphonies, you never quite get a chance to glimpse eternity. Or if you do glimpse it every once in a while, it's the perfect presentation as it flashes past you out the kitchen door.

Cooking—yes, even cooking with latitude—is all so temporary, so here and now. Sometimes you forget that each plate is actually carrying everything you've ever pieced together and called your life.

Ingredients with Latitude

As you've gathered from the introduction, my idea of a pantry is as multinational as my idea of a shopping list is long. Well, not really long, but definitely rich in variety and experience.

In the end, this book isn't about number of ingredients or complexity of techniques—some of my favorite dishes are quite simple. It's about approaching cooking as an adventure, an exploration—and at least part of the attitude required is an openness to interesting new ingredients.

The good news is that, with expansions in domestic produce and fast, affordable access to most exotic items from anywhere on earth, the chef and even the home cook in the suburbs have access to produce, herbs, and spices that a mere generation ago were available only to the most expensive restaurants in the world's largest cities.

The list of such items is never complete, of course, especially since what's "exotic" to one cook might well seem everyday to another. But here's an alphabetical primer on some of my favorites; where and why they found their way into my kitchen; and how I like to see them used. If you haven't done so already, as you get deeper into this book, you may well want to draw up a list of your own. After all, eventually it'll be your cooking—so it will be your latitude.

AHI TUNA: My wife, Kendra, and I went to Hawaii on our honeymoon, so I guess I'm biased in favor of Hawaiian fish because we tasted so many great ones there. "Ahi tuna" is actually redundant, since *ahi* is Hawaiian for tuna. Tuna from Hawaii is one of my favorite fish to use, especially since I prefer it either sushi-raw or barely seared. These days ahi is a name applied to yellowfin tuna, not to the high-fat albacore or to the larger bluefin. Yellowfins can reach up to 300 pounds, with a flesh of light pink and a pronounced tuna flavor—compared to the white and, to my taste, bland albacore. If you ask me, tuna cooked almost any way (except "over") is terrific, from raw to broiled to grilled.

BRICK LEAVES: This ultra-thin prepared pastry dough is airier than phyllo. It is used to make the traditional meat- and cheese-filled turnovers known as some version of "borek."

CAVIAR: Whether it's classically served with its traditional condiments or spooned in small quantity atop the perfect piece of fish, this sieved and lightly salted fish-egg delicacy exists in a food stratosphere all by itself. Not only is it one of the most expensive culinary pleasures available, caviar commands the most respect because nearly all its zealots prefer it just as it is. Toast points, chopped onion, capers, crumbled egg yolk—most of us could set out the display in our sleep. These days, as always, the most esteemed caviar comes from the Caspian Sea shared by Russia and Iran, two countries that long reserved caviar for the ruling class. The most expensive type comes from the beluga sturgeon that swims in the Caspian, with OSETRA, also from sturgeon, and SEVRUGA, a form of sieved and salted sturgeon roe, pulling up right behind.

CELERY ROOT: Also known as celeriac, this root from specially cultivated celery is finally catching on in the United States after holding a place in French cuisine forever. The taste is somewhere between parsley and typical celery, making it nice raw and grated or shredded over a salad. But I've found a lot of other uses for celery root: boiling it, braising it, sautéing it. The leaves of this form of celery cannot be eaten, so the root is usually sold all by itself. It's available between September and May.

CHANTERELLES: This is one of my favorites from among the "wild" or forest mushrooms that have become so central to the modern chef's repertoire. People love wild mushrooms—my diners tell me they do, all the time—and certainly chanterelles play a big part in the passion. Most of them are still being imported from Europe (where the French know them as *girolles*), but increasing numbers are turning up that have been picked along the East Coast or in the Pacific Northwest. They are recognizable for their shape, resembling a trumpet, and their color, ranging from bright yellow to orange. I like to add chanterelles toward the end of any preparation, since they get a little tough if you overcook them. Other wonderful wild mushrooms include morels, porcini, and shiitake. For grilling, it's hard to beat the recently popular portobello.

CONCH: In my restaurant, I've developed quite a following for baby conch, which predictably are a good deal more tender than the grown-up version celebrated in the Caribbean and south Florida. Most people—unless they've been to the islands and eaten either conch fritters or conch salad—know conch more as a shell than as a food. The graceful, bright-hued spiral is the seashell we picture when we dream of that tropical vacation. The conch inside, however, is officially a gastropod mollusk, and a pretty tough one to boot. Most Caribbean conch recipes emphasize the need to tenderize the meat, by either beating it or applying some kind of tenderizer. Look for baby conch and you should find meat that's tender enough. You'll love the cool, clear taste of the sea.

COUSCOUS: Yes, my restaurant does a great job with mashed potatoes and with orzo pasta; but one of the most versatile and delicious starches I've tasted on earth is this granular semolina from North Africa. In that culture, it's a staple that takes many forms, from pungent salad to milky-sweet dessert. Best of all, it gives its name to a full meal, when it's cooked by steaming in a *couscoussiere* and served along with the meat and vegetables prepared in other sections of the same utensil. At Dominique's, couscous might be flavored with anything, but in North Africa you can often tell its national origin by its primary flavoring. Morocco, just across a bit of water from Spain, loves its couscous with saffron, while Algeria loves tomatoes added and Tunisia spices up the whole affair with the hot-pepper sauce called *harissa*.

DAIKON: I think you'll love the sweet, fresh flavor of this oversized Japanese radish. The word in Japanese means "large root," but that's only the beginning of the story. It has a skin ranging from white to black, and crisp white flesh. I've seen daikons that are almost as big as a football. I go for firm, unwrinkled daikons and use them any number of ways, from adding crunch to a salad, to garnishing a plate, to fixing one of my signature dishes, a very Asian Crab and Daikon Roll (page 32).

FOIE GRAS: To previous generations, this fattened goose liver so loved by the French was seen, along with caviar, as the standard of having arrived. After some loss of interest, a new generation of diners has rediscovered foie gras, surely not as a daily indulgence but as exactly what it is—an extraordinary marriage of lush taste and texture. Literally, foie gras means "fat liver," a reference to that part of a goose that's been fed way too much and prevented from exercising. France still produces much of the world's finest foie gras, hailing from the Alsace and Perigord regions, yet many American chefs now pledge their allegiance to foie gras from the Hudson Valley. Like most of the best things in life, foie shouldn't have too much done to it. We chefs have to know when enough is enough—and with delicious foie gras, just a little technique or embellishment goes a long way.

GARAM MASALA: My mother keeps me supplied with this Indian spice mixture, sending regular packages of this and other herbs and spices from the markets in Mauritius to my kitchen in New Orleans. Garam masala is what real Indian cooks (and American cooks who want real Indian flavors) use for "curry" instead of so-called curry powder. It's a blend of up to 12 spices, perhaps including black pepper, cinnamon, coriander, cumin, dried chiles, fennel, mace, nutmeg, and turmeric. The words *garam masala* mean something warm or hot, and that's the element the mix brings to food—both back home in northern India and anywhere an adventurous cook wants to sprinkle some into a pan. Traditionally, you had to find an Indian or at least ethnic market to find garam masala; now it turns up in many supermarkets on the International aisle.

GINGER: Yes, we all know it as ginger root. However, ginger isn't actually a root but a rhizome growing on an underground stem. There would be virtually no Chinese cooking without the flavor of ginger. Still, grated or minced ginger finds itself happy in plenty of dishes that aren't Chinese, even in my restaurant's popular version of New Orleans' barbecued shrimp. I really enjoy the pickled ginger served beside sushi. As most good cooks already know, dried powder ginger is never a substitute for the real thing in savory dishes. It's designed for baking, as in gingerbread or gingersnaps, and does nothing right when you really want fresh ginger.

GOAT CHEESE: Diners who love French cuisine tend to call goat cheese "chevre" and prefer its tart, distinctive flavor to any cheese made with cow's milk. Celebrants of Greek food, though, are likely to talk about feta—the variety of goat cheese found throughout the Greek mainland and the islands, where cows are nearly mythical animals. Call it what you will, I love goat cheese, which figured in one of the earliest of my recipes to attract attention: the Goat Cheese Wrapped in Phyllo with Sweet Onion Fricassee (page 24). There's plenty of variety among goat cheese in this country, with dozens of small, regional cheesemakers trying their hand. Among the French brands, look for Banon, Bucheron, or Montrachet.

KAFFIR LIME: Don't get all wrapped up in this citrus fruit grown in Southeast Asia and Hawaii, since it's the leaves we're going to use time and again. There is a fruit, of course, and its rind can be grated (zested, as we chefs like to say) and used in some interesting way. But, honestly, just buy the leaves. They're bumpy and wrinkled looking, they're a kind of yellow-green, and they look a little like two leaves joined at one end. They possess—and share with whatever they're placed in—a wonderful citrusy aroma reminiscent of lemongrass, that other staple of Southeast Asia's best dishes. Dried kaffir lime leaves can be bought in Asian markets; the fresh leaves are sometimes available as well.

KOBE BEEF: Cooking in the nation that gave the world thick, juicy steak and paraded it before populations a thousand miles from the nearest cow, I'm almost embarrassed to buy beef from Japan. But that's what I do a lot of the time, loving what I taste in beef from the Japanese city of Kobe. The treatment this beef receives (when still in its living form) is extraordinary. The cattle are fed plenty of beer (which I can attest has many nutritional advantages!) and they're even massaged with sake, a pleasure I haven't even had yet. The result is beef that's full of flavor yet very, very tender. Oh yes, did I mention, it's really expensive?

LEMONGRASS: Lovers of Thai and Vietnamese food have already met this herb, notable for the long, grass-like leaves that inspire the name, and the lemony perfume. We usually use only the white part at the bottom of each green stalk. You should peel off the tough outer leaves, then chop up the inside. In any dish based on the flavor profiles of Southeast Asia, you'll find

lemongrass achieves nirvana when used with spring onions, garlic, and coriander.

LETTUCES: In the United States, we all know what the word lettuce used to mean: iceberg. People tell me that iceberg is making a comeback, maybe riding in with Mom's meatloaf and mashed potatoes. But I for one am glad my adopted country has finally gotten around to embracing the vast array of lettuces available. The popularity means more farmers are growing more types of lettuce, so things can only keep getting better. Generally, all lettuces fall into one of four categories: butterhead, crisphead, leaf, and Romaine. Naturally, lettuce is the star of almost any salad, but if you're cooking with a lot of latitude you can turn it into a satisfying soup or wilt it for serving under a fish or poultry entree. As many of the "newer" lettuces have a sharp or peppery taste, do not just count on all lettuces just sitting there like iceberg. A couple of specialty "lettuces" I use in this book are FRISEE, a member of the chicory family with slender, curly leaves, and MACHE, sometimes called "corn salad," with leaves that are dark and have a tangy, nutlike flavor.

MEYER LEMON: A scientist named Frank Meyer promised in the early 1900s to "skim the earth for things good to man." His name is now carried on at least one of the 2,500 or so good things he introduced into the United States. The Meyer, which he brought in from China, is not considered a true lemon. When mature, it shares many of the characteristics of a large orange. Intended first and foremost for use in cooking, its juice has a sweeter flavor than that of most lemons, making it perfect for desserts without the addition of too much sugar. Meyer lemons are grown at the northern end of California's citrus belt.

OSTRICH: Though ostrich the bird is always affectionately featured in travel documentaries about Africa, ostrich the entrée is extremely new in the United States. The main reason for its rise is the proliferation of profit-driven ostrich ranches in this country, most of which are finding greater receptiveness for their meat than emu ranches are finding for theirs. I, for one, featured an ostrich burger with some success when my restaurant opened. Since then, I've come to concentrate on ostrich consommé, which I find rich in flavor and lovely in appearance. The meat can be quite good, I think, attracting not only impressive nutritional numbers but comparisons to lean beef.

SESAME: In my restaurant, sesame takes any number of forms, as you might expect from a chef who loves Asian flavors. The first form is sesame seeds themselves, which can add interest to the crust of almost anything and also star in the graceful Parmesan "fricos" we serve with our Romaine salad. Sesame oil is another terrific Chinese flavor. When you add just a few drops

at the end of cooking, it adds an aroma and a taste that's beyond compare. And finally, there's sesame seed paste, made from roasted seeds and therefore darker than the tahini featured in Middle Eastern cuisines.

SWEETBREADS: The thymus glands not only of veal but sometimes of young lamb, beef, or pork, these "variety meats" seem to be gaining increased popularity among Americans. They've never not been popular in Europe, and they did turn up on menus in this country throughout the nineteenth century. Of course, almost every organ did at that time. There are two sweetbreads per animal, with the larger and rounder one near the heart being most prized and, of course, most expensive. I prefer sweetbreads from milk-fed baby veal, which you can probably find anytime at a specialty meat market. I like sweetbreads cooked any way, from poached to braised to sautéed. But one of the best ways I've ever tasted is described in this book: Sugarcane Brochette of Sweetbreads with Truffled Mashed Potato and Wild Mushroom Jus (page 151).

TRUFFLE: A fortune for a fungus? Yes, more or less. Truffles are indeed a fungus that attaches to tree roots in certain areas of France and Italy. Before they become an expensive delight, however, somebody has to find them underground— a task colorfully carried out by pigs, and sometimes by dogs as well. The idea, considering the price tag, is that the animals do not gobble the truffle but leave it to be oh-so-carefully dug up. When it comes to truffles, there is a bit of a rivalry between black and white and between France and Italy. The black, or dark brown, is pungent in taste and hails from the Perigord and Quercy regions of France, as well as from Umbria in Italy. The white truffle comes from Italy's Piedmont, where of course people claim it's the best in the world. Fresh imported truffles can be found from late fall into the middle of winter. Some of these recipes call for TRUFFLE BUTTER, butter flavored with truffle and herbs, and TRUFFLE OIL, an oil flavored with a bit of truffle that imparts flavor without the expense of buying the fungus itself.

VANILLA: I have to speak about vanilla because it's one the few things Americans enjoy regularly that comes from my part of the world. The Indian Ocean is shared by my island of Mauritius with Madagascar and Reunion, two isles that grow most of the pods used to make real vanilla on earth. Actually, the idea of using the world's only edible orchid came from the Aztecs of Mexico, who were smart enough to pair it with their other great contribution to life as we know it, chocolate. Mexico still produces some vanilla extract, but the real competition for Indian Ocean vanilla comes from Tahiti in French Polynesia. Besides being a hard-to-leave destination, Tahiti grows vanilla that's thicker and darker than the "beans" from anyplace else. Everyone loves vanilla in dessert, whether it's in ice cream, sauce, or custard. Yet quite a few chefs are experimenting with vanilla in savory dishes, and have considerable success pairing it with the sweet meat of lobster.

WASABI: Sushi lovers of the world, unite! In fact, we probably all will, one of these days. Till then, we can appreciate not only the fine Japanese flavors of our favorite sushi but the taste of wasabi mixed in with soy we use for a dipping sauce. Coming from the root of an Asian plant, wasabi is a condiment that's increasingly familiar in creative American cooking. Some people like to call it Japanese horseradish, which I guess is as good a name as any for a root that produces such a sharp-tasting and sinus-clearing additive. Traditionally available only in Asian markets, wasabi has entered the mainstream, turning up at the supermarket in either paste or powder form. There is such a thing as fresh wasabi, available from some specialty produce stores. The root can and should be grated, just like horseradish.

BASICS

‎❧

Oven-Dried Tomatoes

24 PLUM TOMATOES

4 CUPS OLIVE OIL

½ CUP MINCED GARLIC

2 TABLESPOONS GRANULATED SUGAR

2 TABLESPOONS SEA SALT

2 TABLESPOONS CRUSHED BLACK PEPPER

1 BUNCH THYME

Preheat the oven to 150°. Core the tomatoes and slice a cross in the top of each. Blanch the tomatoes in boiling water for about 20 seconds. Drain and peel. Pour the olive oil into a 16 by 24-inch sheet pan. Layer the pan with the tomatoes and cover them with the garlic, sugar, salt, pepper, and thyme. Bake for 15 hours. Store covered in olive oil at all times. It will keep for a week to 10 days.

Oven-Dried Tomato Oil

Prepare the Oven-Dried Tomatoes and drain off the oil from the pan after baking the tomatoes. This oil is the oven-dried tomato oil. It will keep refrigerated for 2 weeks.

Crème Fraîche

1 CUP BUTTERMILK

1 CUP HEAVY CREAM

1 TEASPOON FRESHLY SQUEEZED LEMON JUICE

In a stainless steel mixing bowl, combine the buttermilk, heavy cream, and lemon juice. Cover and leave out at room temperature for 3 days. When thick, you can keep refrigerated for up to 10 days.

Homemade Mayonnaise

2 TABLESPOONS RED WINE VINEGAR

2 TABLESPOONS DIJON MUSTARD

2 EGG YOLKS

1½ CUPS OLIVE OIL

KOSHER OR TABLE SALT

PEPPER

In a mixing bowl, combine the vinegar, mustard, and egg yolks. Stir in the olive oil slowly until the mixture is thoroughly incorporated. Add salt and pepper to taste. Refrigerate. It may be kept in the refrigerator for up to 3 days.

Habanero Oil

4 CUPS PLUS 2 TABLESPOONS GRAPESEED OIL

3 SHALLOTS, PEELED AND CHOPPED

5 HABANERO PEPPERS, SEEDED

1 TEASPOON PEELED AND CHOPPED FRESH GINGER

1 TEASPOON CHOPPED GARLIC

1 TEASPOON CHOPPED FRESH LEMONGRASS

1 BUNCH CILANTRO

1 CUP LIGHT SESAME OIL

Heat 2 tablespoons of the grapeseed oil in a pan over medium heat. Sauté the shallots for 2 minutes. Add the habanero peppers, ginger, garlic, and lemongrass. Sauté for 5 minutes. Add the 4 cups of grapeseed oil and the sesame oil. Simmer for 10 minutes. Add the cilantro and remove from heat. Allow to steep until cool. Strain and keep refrigerated for up to 1 month.

Habanero Vinegar

5 CUPS WHITE WINE VINEGAR

Follow the recipe for Habanero Oil above, except in place of the 4 cups of grapeseed oil and 1 cup of sesame oil use 5 cups white wine vinegar.

Pickling Sauce

*T*his is a basic pickling sauce; however, I've added lemongrass because I believe it gives it a special fresh taste. This pickling sauce is good to have on hand to pickle vegetables which are first air-dried in the sun.

2 CUPS WHITE WINE VINEGAR

2 TABLESPOONS TURMERIC

1 TABLESPOON GARAM MASALA OR CURRY POWDER

¼ CUP FINELY CHOPPED GARLIC

½ CUP PEELED AND FINELY CHOPPED FRESH GINGER

2 TABLESPOONS WHOLE GRAIN MUSTARD

2 TABLESPOONS CAYENNE PEPPER

2 LARGE YELLOW ONIONS, FINELY CHOPPED

1 CUP CHOPPED FRESH CILANTRO

1 TABLESPOON SALT

1 TEASPOON FRESHLY GROUND BLACK PEPPER

2 STALKS LEMONGRASS, FINELY CHOPPED

4 CUPS OLIVE OIL

Mix all the ingredients together except for the olive oil. Allow to marinate for 3 days in the refrigerator. Add the oil and allow to marinate in the refrigerator for an additional 4 days. Strain through a fine sieve. Keep in a sterile container in the refrigerator until ready to use.

Duck Confit

*C*onfit can be made out of any part of the duck, but the legs are the juiciest.

10 DUCK LEGS

3 CUPS RENDERED DUCK FAT (SEE ABOVE)

3 TABLESPOONS CHOPPED GARLIC

1 TABLESPOON KOSHER SALT

1 TABLESPOON CRACKED BLACK PEPPER

½ CUP CHOPPED FRESH THYME

4 SPRIGS OF THYME, FOR GARNISH

To make the duck confit, in a large glass container, coat the duck legs with the garlic, salt, pepper, and chopped thyme. Refrigerate overnight. The next day, heat the rendered duck fat in a large saucepan over medium heat. Submerge the legs in the fat; they should be completely covered. Cook over a low heat — no more than 200° — for 4 to 6 hours. If you use a higher heat to speed things up, the confit will be tough. It is done when the meat is easily removed from the bones.

Leave the meat on the bones until it is needed, as it will keep longer this way. Also, use gloves whenever you handle the confit to avoid contamination. This will also help it keep longer.

Rendered Duck Fat

5 POUNDS DUCK SKIN

Place the duck skin in a saucepan over medium-low heat for 25 to 35 minutes. Do not boil. You know the skin has released all the fat when it is crispy and crackling. Remove from heat and strain through a fine sieve. This can be kept in the refrigerator for up to 6 months. For a true taste treat, use it for sautéing instead of vegetable oil.

STOCKS

Crab Stock

YIELD: ⅓ GALLON

¼ CUP OF OVEN-DRIED TOMATO OIL
(PAGE 2)

6 CARROTS, PEELED AND CHOPPED

4 YELLOW ONIONS, PEELED AND CHOPPED

1 CELERY STALK, CHOPPED

10 OVEN-DRIED TOMATOES (PAGE 2)

5 POUNDS WHOLE BLUE CRABS

1 STALK LEMONGRASS, CHOPPED
(OPTIONAL)

1 GALLON BLOND CHICKEN STOCK
(PAGE 17) OR WATER

2 BAY LEAVES

Heat the oil in a large pot and sauté the carrots, onions, and celery in the oil until they are lightly caramelized. Add the Oven-Dried Tomatoes, blue crabs, and lemongrass and cook for about 10 minutes, stirring to ensure that the crabs absorb the vegetable flavor. Add the chicken stock and bay leaves and bring to a rolling boil for about 20 minutes. Skim the impurities off the top. Remove from the heat, transfer the mixture to a blender, and blend thoroughly. Strain through a cheesecloth-lined strainer into a container. Keep refrigerated for up to 5 days, frozen for up to 6 months.

Note: Water may be used in place of chicken stock; however,
I prefer chicken stock because it packs this recipe with flavor
and richness through the process of layering flavors.

Shrimp Stock

YIELD: 1/3 GALLON

2 TABLESPOONS OLIVE OIL

6 CARROTS, PEELED AND CHOPPED

4 YELLOW ONIONS, PEELED AND CHOPPED

1 CELERY STALK, PEELED

1 GALLON BLOND CHICKEN STOCK
(PAGE 17) OR WATER

3 BAY LEAVES

5 POUNDS SHRIMP HEADS

Heat the oil in a pan and sauté carrots, onions, and celery in the olive oil until they are lightly caramelized. Add the chicken stock and bay leaves and bring to a boil. Add the shrimp heads and return to a boil for 15 minutes. Continuously skim the impurities from the top. Transfer the mixture to a blender or hand mixer and blend thoroughly. Strain through a cheesecloth-lined strainer into a container. Keep refrigerated for up to 5 days, frozen for up to 6 months.

Fish Stock

YIELD: ⅓ GALLON

2 TABLESPOONS OLIVE OIL

6 CARROTS, PEELED AND CHOPPED

4 YELLOW ONIONS, PEELED AND CHOPPED

1 CELERY STALK, PEELED AND CHOPPED

1 LEEK, CHOPPED

1 GALLON WATER

3 BAY LEAVES

5 POUNDS FISH BONES, CLEANED, WITH GILLS AND BLOOD REMOVED

Heat the oil in a pan and sauté the carrots, onions, celery, and leek in the olive oil until lightly caramelized. Add the water and bring to a boil. Add the bay leaves and fish bones. Return to a boil for 10 minutes. Continuously skim the impurities from the top. Strain through a cheesecloth-lined strainer, and transfer to another sauce pot. Return to heat and simmer until reduced by half. Keep refrigerated for up to 5 days, frozen for up to 6 months.

Suggested fish: Dover sole, halibut, John Dory, or snapper.
Use bones with the heads (no gills) and tails only.

Fish Fumet

YIELD: 1 QUART

2 TABLESPOONS OLIVE OIL

6 CARROTS, PEELED AND CHOPPED

4 YELLOW ONIONS, PEELED AND CHOPPED

1 CELERY STALK, PEELED AND CHOPPED

1 LEEK, CHOPPED

2 BOTTLES SAUVIGNON BLANC OR
OTHER DRY WHITE WINE

2 QUARTS WATER

5 POUNDS FISH BONES, CLEANED,

WITH GILLS AND BLOOD REMOVED

2 TABLESPOONS CHOPPED FRESH TARRAGON

2 TABLESPOONS CHOPPED FRESH THYME

2 TABLESPOONS CHOPPED FRESH BASIL

1 TABLESPOON CHOPPED FRESH ROSEMARY

1 TABLESPOON CHOPPED FRESH OREGANO

2 TABLESPOONS CHOPPED FRESH CHERVIL

4 KAFFIR LIME LEAVES

Heat the oil in a pan and sauté the carrots, onions, celery, and leek in the olive oil until lightly caramelized. Add the wine and water and bring to a rolling boil. Immediately add the fish bones and return to a boil for 10 minutes. Continuously skim the impurities from the top. Strain through a cheesecloth-lined strainer into another sauce pot. Add the herbs and lime leaves. Return to low heat and simmer for 3 hours. Strain again and place in a container. Keep refrigerated for up to 5 days, frozen for up to 6 months.

Suggested fish: Dover sole, halibut, John Dory, or snapper.
Use bones with the heads (no gills) and tails only.

Lobster Stock

YIELD: ⅓ GALLON

¾ CUP OVEN-DRIED
TOMATO OIL (PAGE 2)

5 POUNDS LOBSTER TORSOS

6 CARROTS, PEELED AND CHOPPED

4 YELLOW ONIONS, PEELED AND CHOPPED

2 CELERY STALKS, CHOPPED

2 LEEKS, CHOPPED

2 CUPS DRY SHERRY

1 CUP OVEN-DRIED TOMATOES (PAGE 2)

1 GALLON BLOND CHICKEN STOCK
(PAGE 17) OR WATER

4 KAFFIR LIME LEAVES

1 BUNCH PARSLEY

Preheat the oven to 350°. Coat the bottom of a large roasting pan with ¼ cup of the Oven-Dried Tomato Oil. Layer the lobster torsos in the pan and roast for 15 minutes. Remove the pan from the oven, remove the lobster torsos from the pan, and set aside. (The torsos will be used later for the stock.)

Place the roasting pan on a burner over medium heat. Heat the remaining ½ cup of oil in the pan. Add the carrots, onions, celery, and leeks. Stir the vegetables until lightly caramelized, approximately 10 minutes. Deglaze the pan with the sherry and stir to incorporate. Add the Oven-Dried Tomatoes and stir to blend. Transfer the mixture to a large stock pot and add the roasted lobster torsos, chicken stock, lime leaves, and parsley. Bring to a rolling boil and boil for approximately 20 minutes. Remove from heat and transfer to a blender. Blend the mixture until it is puréed. Strain through a cheesecloth-lined strainer and cool. Keep refrigerated for up to 5 days, frozen for up to 6 months.

Langoustine Stock

¾ CUP OVEN-DRIED TOMATO OIL (PAGE 2)

5 POUNDS LANGOUSTINE HEADS

6 CARROTS, PEELED AND CHOPPED

4 YELLOW ONIONS, PEELED AND CHOPPED

2 CELERY STALKS, CHOPPED

2 LEEKS, CHOPPED

2 CUPS DRY VERMOUTH

1 CUP PURÉED OVEN-DRIED TOMATOES (PAGE 2)

1 GALLON BLOND CHICKEN STOCK (PAGE 17) OR WATER

4 KAFFIR LIME LEAVES

1 BUNCH PARSLEY

Preheat the oven to 350°. Coat the bottom of a large roasting pan with ¼ cup of the Oven-Dried Tomato Oil. Place a single layer of the langoustine heads in the bottom of the pan and roast for 15 minutes. Remove the pan from the oven and set the langoustine heads aside. (The heads will be used later for the stock.)

Add the remaining ½ cup of oil to the roasting pan and heat over a medium flame. Add the carrots, onions, celery, and leeks. Stir the vegetables until lightly caramelized, approximately 10 minutes. Deglaze the pan with the vermouth and stir to incorporate. Add the Oven-Dried Tomato purée and blend. Transfer the mixture to a large stock pot and add the roasted langoustine heads, chicken stock, lime leaves, and parsley. Bring to a rolling boil and boil for approximately 20 minutes. Remove from heat and transfer to a blender. Blend the mixture until it is puréed. Strain through a cheesecloth-lined strainer and cool. Keep refrigerated for up to 5 days, frozen for up to 6 months.

Crawfish Stock

YIELD: ⅓ GALLON

¼ CUP OLIVE OIL	5 POUNDS LIVE CRAWFISH
6 CARROTS, PEELED AND CHOPPED	4 CLOVES GARLIC
4 WHITE ONIONS, PEELED AND CHOPPED	10 OVEN-DRIED TOMATOES (PAGE 2)
1 CELERY STALK, PEELED AND CHOPPED	1 GALLON WATER
2 LEEKS, CHOPPED	3 BAY LEAVES

Heat the oil in a medium pot and sauté the carrots, onions, celery, and leeks. Add the live crawfish and garlic cloves and sauté until lightly caramelized. Stir in the Oven-Dried Tomatoes. Add the water and bring to a boil. Add the bay leaves and boil for 20 minutes. Continuously skim the impurities from the top. Stir to blend thoroughly and strain through a cheesecloth-lined strainer.

Blond Chicken Stock

YIELDS ABOUT 1 QUART

2 TABLESPOONS VEGETABLE OIL

6 CELERY STALKS, CHOPPED

3 ONIONS, PEELED AND CHOPPED

10 POUNDS CHICKEN BONES

2 CARROTS, PEELED AND CHOPPED

1 GALLON COLD WATER

In a large stock pot, heat the vegetable oil and sauté the onions, carrots and celery for 3 minutes over medium heat. Add the chicken bones and cold water. Lower the heat and simmer for 3 hours. Frequently skim the fat and impurities from the top. Strain through a cheesecloth-lined strainer into another sauce pot, and simmer until reduced to 1 quart. Keep refrigerated for up to 5 days; keep frozen for up to 6 months.

Note: For a darker chicken stock, roast the chicken bones in a 325° oven for 35 minutes before using in this recipe.

Duck Stock

Follow recipe for Chicken Stock (above), substituting duck bones for the chicken bones.

Lamb Stock

3 TABLESPOONS TOMATO PASTE   15 POUNDS LAMB BONES

Preheat the oven to 350°. In a baking pan, spread the tomato paste over the lamb bones. Roast the bones for 35 minutes.

Follow the recipe for Blond Chicken Stock (page 17), substituting the 15 pounds of roasted lamb bones for the chicken bones.

Rabbit Stock

Follow the recipe for Lamb Stock, substituting rabbit bones for the lamb bones.

Veal Stock

Follow the recipe for Lamb Stock, substituting veal bones for the lamb bones.

Venison Stock

1 POUND MUSHROOMS

Follow the recipe for Lamb Stock, substituting venison bones for the lamb bones. Add the mushrooms with the vegetables.

Vegetable Stock

YIELDS ABOUT 1 QUART

3 TABLESPOONS OVEN-DRIED TOMATO OIL (PAGE 2)

6 OVEN-DRIED TOMATOES (PAGE 2)

1 POUND CREMINI MUSHROOMS

2 LEEKS, CLEANED AND CHOPPED

1 FENNEL BULB, CHOPPED

8 CELERY STALKS

3 ONIONS, PEELED AND CHOPPED

4 CARROTS, PEELED AND CHOPPED

4 QUARTS COLD WATER

In a large stock pot, heat the oil and sauté all the vegetables over medium heat for about 7 minutes. Add the cold water, bring to a boil, then simmer for 2 hours. Strain and simmer until reduced to 1 quart. Keep refrigerated for up to 5 days, frozen for up to 6 months.

APPETIZERS

Lobster and Foie Gras Terrine
22

Goat Cheese Wrapped in Phyllo
24

Louisiana Crawfish
with a Spicy Aioli
26

Grilled Baby Conch
28

Lobster and Mango Salad
30

Crab and Daikon Roll
32

Marinated Roma Tomatoes
34

Truffled Cappuccino of
White Water Clams
36

Ahi Tuna and Crispy Pineapple
Mille-Feuille
37

Baby Conch and
Spiny Lobster Salad
39

Seared Foie Gras and Brick Leaves
41

Marinated Heirloom Tomatoes
42

Ginger-Charred Kobe Beef "Tartare"
43

Turmeric-Crusted Blue Marlin
45

Truffled "Oeuf Brouillé"
with Foie Gras
47

Green Papaya au Gratin
48

Lobster and Foie Gras Terrine
with Chanterelle and Pistachio Vinaigrette

I guess you could call this my version of "surf and turf," as I love to pair foie gras with all types of seafood, from tuna to scallops. My favorite marriage has to be foie gras and lobster, which come together in this terrine. The chanterelle and pistachio vinaigrette, I've found, adds a pleasantly creamy texture to the finished dish.

SERVES 10

Lobster and Foie Gras Terrine

1 GALLON VEGETABLE STOCK (PAGE 19)

4 (1-POUND) MAINE LOBSTERS

1½ POUND FOIE GRAS

1 POUND CHANTERELLE MUSHROOMS

KOSHER OR TABLE SALT

BLACK PEPPER

1 TABLESPOON FINELY CHOPPED CHERVIL

BABY ARUGULA, FOR GARNISH

Chanterelle and Pistachio Vinaigrette

1 POUND CHANTERELLE MUSHROOMS

1 CUP OSTRICH CONSOMMÉ (PAGE 60)

½ CUP GRAPESEED OIL

¼ CUP PISTACHIO OIL

2 TABLESPOONS MERLOT VINEGAR

KOSHER OR TABLE SALT

COARSELY GROUND BLACK PEPPER

To prepare the terrine, bring the stock to a rolling boil in a large stock pot. Add the lobsters and boil for five minutes. Remove the lobsters and allow to cool. Shell them by removing the tail and claw meats, being careful to keep in whole pieces.

Slice the foie gras into ¼-inch slices and quickly sear both sides in a cast iron skillet on high heat. Push the fat drippings through a fine sieve to remove impurities and set aside to cool. Set the foie gras aside on a cooling rack.

Reserve half the fat for assembling the terrine and return half the fat to the skillet. Sauté the mushrooms in the fat over medium heat for approximately 8 minutes, seasoning with salt and pepper. Remove from the heat, add the chervil, and allow to cool.

To assemble the terrine, line a rectangular terrine mold with plastic wrap. Layer the chanterelles, lobster meat, and foie gras. Pour the remaining foie gras oil over each layer to moisten and press down each layer before adding the next. When the terrine is filled to the top, press down with a weight and refrigerate for 6 hours.

To make the vinaigrette, in a blender, purée the mushrooms with the consommé until smooth. Add the grapeseed oil, pistachio oil, and merlot vinegar. Season with salt and pepper, and blend until thoroughly emulsified.

To serve, slice the terrine into 1-inch-thick slices. Place on individual serving plates and drizzle with vinaigrette. Garnish with arugula.

Wine notes: A chardonnay is perfect with this terrine, as long as it does not have too much oak. My suggestions would include those of Grgich Hills or Matanzas Creek.

Goat Cheese Wrapped in Phyllo
with a Sweet Onion Fricassee

This is one of my best-received dishes, going back to my days in London.
In those days, I was experimenting with various preserves (and no doubt tasting a
lot of chutneys in London's thousands of Indian restaurants). I stumbled onto
these slow-cooked onions with all their natural sweetness, and I loved the intensity.
In my restaurant kitchen, the process of preparing the onions takes 72 hours. But
we prepare 200 pounds of it at a time, put it in large plastic containers, and keep
it for up to 6 months in the refrigerator before using it. For this book,
I've reworked the method to be much quicker, with satisfying results.

SERVES 6

Sweet Onion Fricassee

10 WHITE ONIONS, SLICED

1 CUP BALSAMIC VINEGAR

½ CUP HONEY

Goat Cheese Wrapped in Phyllo

12 OUNCES GOAT CHEESE

1 BOX PHYLLO DOUGH

2 OUNCES CLARIFIED BUTTER

½ CUP HONEY

1 CUP BALSAMIC VINEGAR

ARUGULA FOR GARNISH

To prepare the fricassee, put the onions in a large sauce pot set on low heat, and cook for 4 hours in their natural juices. Refrigerate overnight.

On the day of serving, cook the onions in a large sauce pot on medium heat for another 2 hours, until the onions reach a jam consistency. Add the balsamic vinegar and honey to the sauce pot and reduce over medium heat, stirring often, for approximately 2 hours. The mixture should have a thick, dry consistency. Allow to cool.

To prepare the goat cheese wrapped in phyllo, preheat the oven to 300°. Divide the goat cheese into 6 equal portions, approximately 2 ounces each. Layer 4 sheets of phyllo dough, brushing clarified butter over each layer. Cut the stack of 4 sheets in half; each half will make one serving. Repeat the process two more times: layering 4 sheets, brushing with butter, and cutting in half.

To assemble each serving, place a portion of the goat cheese in the middle of one stack of phyllo dough. Add a tablespoon of the onion fricassee and wrap the phyllo around the filling, gathering at the top and twisting to secure (like a beggar's purse). Fill and secure the remaining five servings. Place on a baking sheet and bake for 5 to 6 minutes. Transfer to serving plates.

Mix the honey into the vinegar and drizzle a small amount over each phyllo purse. Garnish with arugula.

Wine notes: I would suggest a white wine from the Loire Valley,
especially the Sancerre from Lucien Crochet.

Louisiana Crawfish
with a Spicy Aioli and Vine-Ripe Tomatoes

Of course, coming to New Orleans, I had to create at least one dish using the plump crawfish tails so important to Creole and Cajun cooking. This one combines the favored shellfish of southern Louisiana with the mild yet savory aioli of southern France. Especially during the long, hot summers, this is a big hit in my restaurant. For this recipe, the crawfish tails may be purchased already peeled, cooked, and packaged in their own liquid.

SERVES 8

¼ CUP DICED GREEN LEEK LEAVES, GREEN PARTS ONLY

1 TABLESPOON UNSALTED BUTTER

1 RED BELL PEPPER, FINELY CHOPPED

1 POUND CRAWFISH TAILS, PEELED AND COOKED, DRAINED

1 TEASPOON CHILI POWDER

2 CELERY STALKS, DICED

1 LARGE DILL PICKLE, DICED

1 MEDIUM RED ONION, SLICED

½ TABLESPOON CELERY SALT

1 TEASPOON PAPRIKA

1 TEASPOON CHOPPED FRESH GARLIC

3 TABLESPOONS HOMEMADE MAYONNAISE (PAGE 3)

1 TABLESPOON FRESHLY SQUEEZED LEMON JUICE

4 VINE-RIPE TOMATOES, SLICED, FOR GARNISH

BASIL SPRIGS, FOR GARNISH

Sauté the leeks in butter over medium heat until golden. Add the red bell pepper and crawfish tails. Sauté for 8 minutes or until the liquid evaporates. Stir in the chili powder. Refrigerate.

In a bowl, combine the celery, pickle, onion, celery salt, paprika, garlic, mayonnaise, and lemon juice. Add the crawfish mixture, and mix well.

Center a 2½-inch-tall circle mold on a serving plate, fill it to the top, and remove the mold. Garnish with tomato slices and fresh basil sprigs.

Wine notes: Rieslings and Gewürztraminers from Germany
go great with this dish.

Grilled Baby Conch

with Kaffir-Lime-Leaf–Braised Hearts of Palm and Pistachio Lobster Emulsion

If you're like me, you've enjoyed several variations on conch in the Caribbean, but I was also lucky enough to grow up eating conch on my home island of Mauritius. To make this great starter, I begin with the tender farm-raised conch of the Turks and Caicos Islands. They're sweeter in taste than the full-grown conch pulled from the sea. The hearts of palm give this dish a nice summery snap.

SERVES 6

Braised Hearts of Palm

2 CUPS LOBSTER STOCK (PAGE 14)

1⅓ CUPS COCONUT MILK

2 KAFFIR LIME LEAVES, JULIENNED

½ TEASPOON SEA SALT

½ TEASPOON FRESHLY CRUSHED BLACK PEPPER

1 POUND HEARTS OF PALM

Pistachio Lobster Emulsion

2 CUPS LOBSTER STOCK (PAGE 14)

½ CUP PISTACHIO OIL

½ CUP GRAPESEED OIL

SEA SALT

FRESHLY CRUSHED BLACK PEPPER

Conch

24 BABY CONCH

4 CUPS COLD WATER

2 TEASPOONS SALT

1 TEASPOON FRESHLY CRUSHED BLACK PEPPER

PISTACHIO OIL FOR THE GRILL

To make the braised hearts of palm, bring the lobster stock and coconut milk to a simmer in a large saucepan over medium heat. Add the lime leaves, salt, pepper, and hearts of palm. Decrease the heat and simmer for 25 minutes. Drain the hearts of palm, discarding the liquid, and let cool. Once cool, julienne the hearts of palm.

To make the emulsion, bring the lobster stock to a boil in a medium size sauce pan over high heat. Cook until reduced by one third, approximately 10 to 12 minutes. Remove from the heat and let cool. Transfer the lobster stock reduction to a blender and while pulsing, gradually add the pistachio and grapeseed oils until thoroughly incorporated. Add salt and pepper to taste.

To prepare the conch, flatten them with a mallet. In a large square glass container, place the flattened conch in a single layer. Add the salt and pepper to the cold water and pour over the conch. Cover and refrigerate until ready to grill. Prepare the grill surface by brushing with pistachio oil. Grill the conch for approximately 15 seconds on each side until lightly browned.

To assemble each serving, place approximately 1 heaping tablespoon of the braised, julienned hearts of palm on the center of a plate. Place 4 grilled conch around the hearts of palm. Drizzle with lobster emulsion. Serve immediately.

Wine notes: To take this dish to the tropics—where I believe it needs to be— pick up a well-balanced sauvignon blanc from Matanzas Creek. And since I've cooked grilled baby conch at this winery in Sonoma County, I know their chardonnay works well with it too.

Lobster and Mango Salad
with Lobster Coral and Meyer Lemon Emulsion

This dish comes out best when the mangoes you select are a little less than ripe—orange, but not at all mushy. The lobster coral or roe—found only on the female lobster—supplies a profound sea flavor, while the grapeseed oil used in the emulsion takes on a beautiful bright red color.

SERVES 8

8 (1-POUND) LIVE,
FEMALE MAINE LOBSTERS

1 GALLON VEGETABLE STOCK (PAGE 19)

Lobster Coral Emulsion

¼ CUP FRESHLY SQUEEZED
LEMON JUICE

1 TABLESPOON LEMON ZEST

2 CUPS LOBSTER STOCK (PAGE 14)

2 CUPS GRAPESEED OIL

LOBSTER CORAL (ROE)

KOSHER OR TABLE SALT

PEPPER

Mango Salad

4 MANGOES

1 TEASPOON LEMON ZEST

3 TEASPOONS LOBSTER CORAL

1 MEYER LEMON, JUICED

To prepare the lobsters, bring the vegetable stock to a boil. Add the lobsters and boil for 5 minutes. Remove the lobster meat from the shells, reserving the coral for the emulsion. Refrigerate the meat and the coral. Reserve the lobster head and tail for garnish. Pull the torso out of the shell. Add the lobster torso to the stock. Continue to boil the stock, uncovered, for about 20 minutes, until it is reduced by half. Transfer the stock to a blender and blend thoroughly. Strain the blended mixture. Return to the stock pot over high heat and simmer until reduced to 2 cups of lobster stock (for use in the emulsion). Allow to cool.

To prepare the emulsion, first set aside 3 teaspoons of the lobster coral for the salad. In a blender, emulsify the remaining coral with all the other emulsion ingredients except the salt and pepper. Be sure to add the grapeseed oil gradually. Season with salt and pepper to taste.

To prepare the salad, peel and julienne the mangoes using a Japanese mandoline, a slicer sold in cookware shops. Place the mango in large stainless mixing bowl and add the lemon zest, lobster coral, and lemon juice. Mix together.

To assemble each serving, place a ring mold on the center of the plate and fill it with mango salad. Arrange the meat of one lobster around the salad, with the tail at the 6 o'clock position and head at 12 o'clock. Drizzle lobster coral emulsion over the lobster meat and salad.

Wine notes: Try a Viognier from my friends at Rideau Vineyard in
Santa Ynez Valley. The 1999 reserve will complement this dish
and blend very well with the coral emulsion.

Crab and Daikon Roll
with Rosemary-Ginger Sauce

*H*ere's a cooling summer dish that I always envision people enjoying by the pool, though it's wonderful in my restaurant—or your dining room—as well. The sweetness of the crabmeat is happy to spend time with the crispness of the daikon, all with a dipping sauce that looks like caramel.

SERVES 4

Rosemary-Ginger Sauce

2 CLOVES GARLIC

1 TABLESPOON CHOPPED
FRESH ROSEMARY

1 TABLESPOON HONEY

½ CUP LIGHT SOY SAUCE

1 JALAPEÑO PEPPER, SEEDED

2 (1 BY 2-INCH) PIECES PEELED
FRESH GINGER

1 CUP GRAPESEED OIL

Crab and Daikon Roll

4 PIECES RICE PAPER

1 LARGE CARROT, FINELY JULIENNED

½ MEDIUM DAIKON, FINELY JULIENNED

¼ CUP COOKED AND CLEANED JUMBO
LUMP CRABMEAT

¼ CUP COOKED AND CLEANED CRAB
CLAW MEAT

To prepare the sauce, purée the garlic, rosemary, honey, soy sauce, jalapeño pepper, and ginger in a blender. Slowly add the grapeseed oil and emulsify.

To prepare the roll, soften each piece of rice paper in a bowl of hot water for approximately 10 seconds. Place on a clean towel until pliable. Reserving 4 loose tablespoons of the carrot and daikon for garnish, layer the ingredients onto the sheets of rice paper, starting with carrots, then daikon, jumbo crabmeat, and claw meat. Roll each up and seal by wetting the edge.

To serve, cut each roll on the bias into 3 pieces. Place a small amount of the reserved carrots and daikon on the center of the plate. Stack the rolls on top and drizzle with the sauce. Serve immediately.

Wine notes: Chablis and Muscadet are different French wines—both light, crisp, and known for their citrus flavors. Either would be great with this roll.

Marinated Roma Tomatoes
with Micro Greens, Crumbled Goat Cheese, Tapenade, and Basil-Mint Oil

The result of this recipe is a salad with a fresh herbal flavor all around, which goes well with the sweetness of the tomatoes and the creaminess of the goat cheese.

SERVES 8

8 RED ROMA TOMATOES,
SLICED INTO 6 SLICES

8 YELLOW ROMA TOMATOES,
SLICED INTO 6 SLICES

½ POUND MICRO-GREEN LETTUCES

3 TABLESPOONS CRUMBLED GOAT CHEESE

COARSELY GROUND BLACK PEPPER

SEA SALT

Tapenade

½ CUP KALAMATA OLIVES, PITTED

½ CUP NIÇOISE OLIVES, PITTED

½ CUP EXTRA-VIRGIN OLIVE OIL

10 BASIL LEAVES

1 TEASPOON CHOPPED FRESH GARLIC

1 TEASPOON CAPERS

Basil-Mint Oil

1 CUP OLIVE OIL

10 BASIL LEAVES

5 MINT LEAVES

2 SPRIGS THYME

2 TEASPOONS CHOPPED FRESH GARLIC

To make the tapenade, purée all the ingredients together in a food processor for about 2 minutes, until coarsely chopped. Set aside.

To make the basil-mint oil, combine the ingredients in a stainless-steel mixing bowl. In a sauté pan over low heat, bring the mixture to a quick boil. Remove from the heat immediately and cool. Strain the mixture into a glass container.

In a stainless-steel mixing bowl, season the tomato slices with the pepper and salt. Add ½ cup of the basil-mint oil to cover. Marinate for 1 hour at room temperature.

To assemble each serving, place one teaspoon of the tapenade on the center of the plate, spreading to form a thin layer. Arrange 6 red tomato slices and 6 yellow tomato slices in a circle, alternating colors and overlapping. Place 1 ounce of the micro-green lettuces in the center of the tomato circle and sprinkle with crumbled goat cheese. Drizzle with the remaining basil-mint oil and serve.

Wine notes: There's no vinegar used in this salad or its dressing, so the wine pairing is a bit easier than usual. There is a certain acidity, however, provided by the tapenade. I'd recommend an Oregon Pinot Blanc such as the Bethel Heights, for its crisp freshness and high acidity.

Truffled Cappuccino of
White Water Clams

*T*he whimsical reference to the Italian coffee drink reflects the good luck of these clams to find themselves in a velvety white froth. I prefer white water clams from Washington state, which are about the same size as those from New England but a little less chewy. The truffle taste goes nicely with the beurre blanc used to produce the froth.

SERVES 4

3 TABLESPOONS TRUFFLE BUTTER, SUCH AS URBANI

2 CUPS HEAVY WHIPPING CREAM

2 SHALLOTS, FINELY DICED

1 TEASPOON FINELY CHOPPED FRESH

GARLIC

1 CUP LOBSTER STOCK (PAGE 14)

40 WHITE WATER CLAMS

¼ OUNCE FRESH TRUFFLES, SHAVED FOR GARNISH

Melt the truffle butter in a medium saucepan over low heat. Add the cream and whisk until stiff. Set aside.

In a medium stock pot over high heat, combine the shallots, garlic, and lobster stock. Bring to a boil. Add the clams and cook until the clams open, approximately 5 minutes. Remove the clams and divide among 4 bowls, 10 in each.

Strain the lobster and clam liquid and transfer it to a blender. Add the truffle butter—cream mixture and purée until frothy, and then pour it over the clams. Garnish with the fresh truffle shavings.

Wine notes: With this one, I really enjoy the Puligny Montrachet, a white burgundy. Many believe the world's best white wines hail from this region.

Ahi Tuna and Crispy Pineapple Mille-Feuille

with Soy-Ginger Vinaigrette

You might call this a simple tartare of tuna—but only if you don't know what an exotic taste and texture the thin slices of dried pineapple bring to the table. A bit of acidity comes from the lime juice, while a bit of the tang comes from the ginger.

SERVES 4

Pineapple Mille-Feuille

1 FRESH PINEAPPLE, PEELED

Soy-Ginger Vinaigrette

2 TABLESPOONS PEELED AND DICED
FRESH GINGER

1 TABLESPOON DICED FRESH GARLIC

2 TABLESPOONS FRESHLY SQUEEZED
LIME JUICE

¼ CUP SOY SAUCE

2 TABLESPOONS DICED SHALLOTS

1 TABLESPOON SESAME OIL

¼ CUP GRAPESEED OIL

Tuna

2 CUPS SUSHI-GRADE TUNA, DICED

½ CUP DICED RED AND GREEN
BELL PEPPER

¼ CUP DICED RED ONION

1 CUCUMBER, NOT PEELED, SLICED THIN

To make the mille-feuille, preheat the oven to 200°. Slice the pineapple into paper-thin slices and arrange on a baking sheet. Bake for 2 hours until crispy like potato chips.

Note: When removing the pineapple from the oven, turn over baking sheet right away or the pineapple will stick to the tray. They will be soft at first but become crisp a few minutes later.

To make the vinaigrette, in a stainless-steel mixing bowl combine the ginger, garlic, lime juice, soy sauce, shallots, and sesame and grapeseed oils. Cover and chill for 1 hour.

To serve, in a stainless steel mixing bowl, combine the tuna, red and green peppers, onion, and ½ cup of the vinaigrette. Arrange the cucumber slices, slightly overlapping, in a circle at the center of a serving plate. Place a ring mold in the center on top of the cucumbers and fill by layering first pineapple chips, then the tuna mixture, repeating both layers, and ending with a top layer of pineapple chips. Drizzle vinaigrette over the cucumber slices. Remove the ring mold and serve.

Wine notes: I think this dish, with its crunch and sweetness, deserves an Alsatian pinot blanc, like Domaine Schlumberger.

Baby Conch and Spiny Lobster with Green Papaya Salad

I was inspired to create this starter by my adventures in Southeast Asia, where several of the flavors featured here feel right at home. The conch itself is simply grilled, but it gains interest from the crisp-tart green papaya and the kalamansi juice, an Asian citrus fruit that is a cross between an orange and a lime, in which the papaya is marinated.

SERVES 4

Vinaigrette

⅓ CUP FRESH COCONUT MILK

1 TEASPOON RICE VINEGAR

1 TEASPOON PALM SUGAR

2 KAFFIR LIME LEAVES

2 TABLESPOONS FISH SAUCE

2 TABLESPOONS PEANUT OIL

2 CLOVES GARLIC, CRUSHED
AND FINELY CHOPPED

1 RED CHILI, SEEDED AND FINELY
CHOPPED

1 TABLESPOON KALAMANSI JUICE OR
FRESHLY SQUEEZED LEMON JUICE

Papaya Salad

1 GREEN PAPAYA, PEELED, SEEDED,
AND JULIENNED

1 LARGE HOTHOUSE CUCUMBER,
SEEDED AND JULIENNED

1 MEDIUM CARROT, PEELED AND
JULIENNED

½ RED ONION, JULIENNED

¼ CUP JULIENNED SCALLIONS

1 CUP GARLIC ROOT
(UNDERGROUND GARLIC SPROUTS)
(OPTIONAL)

4 JAMBO WATER APPLES

4 BABY COCONUTS

(Baby Conch and Spiny Lobster continued)

Conch and Lobster

2 (1½ TO 2-POUND) LIVE OR STEAMED
SPINY LOBSTERS

16 BABY CONCH

CRUSHED BLACK PEPPER

SEA SALT

¼ CUP CRUSHED PEANUTS, FOR GARNISH

To prepare the vinaigrette, blanch the lime leaves in boiling water for 5 seconds, cool, and finely chop. In a sauté pan over medium heat, bring the coconut milk, rice vinegar, palm sugar, and lime leaves to a simmer for 1 minute. Cool. Add the fish sauce, peanut oil, garlic, red chili, and kalamansi juice. Stir and set aside.

To make the salad, toss all ingredients together in a stainless-steel mixing bowl. Add 1 cup of the vinaigrette and toss again. Chill.

To prepare the conch and lobster, lightly oil and preheat the grill. Cut each lobster in half, leaving the head on. Brush the inside with vinaigrette. Season with crushed black pepper and sea salt. Grill, meat side down, for approximately 5 minutes, then for 3 more minutes shell side down.

Flatten the conch with a mallet by hitting it once on the back. Season with crushed black pepper and sea salt. Grill for approximately 15 seconds on each side.

To assemble each serving, place a fourth of the salad on the center of the plate. Lay 4 pieces of conch on the salad. Place a lobster half across the plate. Garnish with crushed peanuts.

Wine notes: I suggest a Riesling from Halbrocken,
specifically the Robert Weil.

Seared Foie Gras and Brick Leaves on Kumquat and Late Harvest Jus

The crispy brick leaves add the right touch to the lush foie gras, making it a bit like a napoleon. The dish cries out for something tart—the kumquat preserves.

SERVES 4

8 OUNCES FOIE GRAS, CUT INTO
1-OUNCE PORTIONS

Kumquat Preserves

16 KUMQUATS

5 CUPS LATE-HARVEST CHARDONNAY

2 CUPS GRANULATED SUGAR

1 CUP VEAL STOCK (PAGE 18)
REDUCED BY ⅓

SALT

PEPPER

BRICK LEAVES

4 SPRIGS OF THYME, FOR GARNISH

To make the preserves, simmer the kumquats, chardonnay, and sugar in a saucepan over low heat for 3 hours, without letting it boil. Remove the kumquats, halve, pit, and set aside. Taste the liquid and add more sugar if too tart. Bring to a boil over high heat for 20 minutes, until reduced to 1 cup. Add the reduced veal stock and simmer until reduced by half, to make the jus. Return the kumquat halves to the jus.

To prepare the foie gras, heat a sauté pan over high heat and sear 20 to 25 seconds per side. Remove the foie gras from the pan. Deglaze the pan with 1 cup of the kumquat jus.

To assemble, ladle 4 tablespoons of the jus with kumquat pieces onto a plate. Stack a brick leaf on top of the kumquats, layering foie gras and more brick leaves. Garnish with thyme.

Wine notes: Any of several late-harvest wines come to mind for pairing with this appetizer. Apart from a great Sauternes, my favorite is Dolce from California. Try the wonderful 1996, with its big nectarine flavor.

Marinated Heirloom Tomatoes, Mâche Lettuce with Shaved Botarga, and Oven-Dried Tomato Oil

This simple, yet amazing salad pays tribute to all those farmers who have perfected the growing of vegetables, such as Farmer Lee Jones at Farmer Jones in Ohio. Try to get as many kinds of tomatoes as possible as each has a unique taste. The delicious mâche gives the tomatoes a herbal creaminess, and the Botarga adds the perfect finish of clean saltiness.

SERVES 4

16 FRESH HEIRLOOM TOMATOES

4 OUNCES MÂCHE LETTUCE

½ CUP OVEN-DRIED TOMATO OIL
(PAGE 2)

1 OUNCE BOTARGA (TUNA CAVIAR),
FOR GARNISH

For each serving, slice 4 tomatoes and place in a circle around the center of the plate with edges overlapping. Place 1 ounce of mâche lettuce in the center.

Shave the botarga with a potato peeler and sprinkle one quarter of the shavings over each portion of tomato. Drizzle each serving with 2 tablespoons of the oil and serve.

Wine notes: I recommend the 1992 Grgich Hill Carneros selection chardonnay. It provides you with the perfect flavor and acidity this dish requires.

Ginger-Charred Kobe Beef "Tartare" with Pickled Legumes, Green Papaya, and Indonesian Sweet Soy Sauce

In this Americanized version of beef tartare, the charring contributes a mild smoky flavor that most people find appealing. Between the pickled vegetables and the Indonesian soy sauce, the sweet and sour balance at the heart of Asian cuisine works to perfection. Ketjap manis, available in Asian markets, is a thick, dark Indonesian sauce that is similar to soy but more complex. Sambal Oelek, also available in Asian markets, is, at its simplest, a combination of hot peppers, brown sugar, and salt.

SERVES 4

1 POUND KOBE BEEF TENDERLOIN

1 CUCUMBER, THINLY SLICED

1 GREEN PAPAYA, FINELY JULIENNED

Indonesian Sweet Soy Sauce

¼ CUP SOY SAUCE

2 TABLESPOONS PEELED, MINCED FRESH GINGER

2 TABLESPOONS MINCED GARLIC

¼ CUP KETJAP MANIS

1 TABLESPOON RICE VINEGAR

¼ CUP SESAME OIL

½ CUP GRAPESEED OIL

1 TEASPOON SAMBAL OELEK

½ TABLESPOON HONEY

Pickled Legumes

1 CUP RICE VINEGAR

1 TEASPOON TURMERIC

1 TEASPOON DICED FRESH SHALLOTS

1 TEASPOON DICED PICKLED GINGER

1 TEASPOON CHOPPED FRESH GARLIC

1 TEASPOON GARAM MASALA OR CURRY POWDER

1 CUP SESAME OIL

1 CUP PEANUT OIL

1 CUP YELLOW WAX BEANS

1 CUP HARICOTS VERTS

To prepare the sauce, blend all the ingredients together in a blender.

To prepare the pickled legumes, in a large stainless-steel mixing bowl combine the rice vinegar, turmeric, shallots, ginger, garlic, and garam masala. Heat the two oils in a sauté pan on high heat. Reduce to medium heat and carefully add the rice vinegar mixture to the oil. Add the wax beans and haricots verts and cook for 3 minutes. Set aside to cool. Dice the legumes.

Marinate the beef in ¾ cup of the sauce for 2 hours in the refrigerator. Reserve the remaining sauce. Heat a cast-iron skillet over very high heat. Sear the beef on all sides until charred. Remove from the heat, cool, and dice. Mix with the diced pickled legumes in a stainless-steel mixing bowl.

To serve, place a 2½-inch-high ring mold in the middle of the plate. Arrange the cucumber slices around the outside of the ring mold. Fill the mold by layering half of the julienned papaya on the bottom in a thin layer, then the marinated beef, then the pickled legumes. Top with the remaining papaya. Drizzle the remaining sweet soy sauce on the cucumber slices. Remove the ring mold and serve.

Wine notes: I would suggest an Austrian Pinot Blanc,
such as the Heinrich Weissburgunder.

Turmeric-Crusted Blue Marlin with Celery-Root Slaw, Wasabi Crème Fraîche, and Plum-Wine Vinaigrette

*M*y home island of Mauritius is actually one of the great game-fishing destinations on earth, a fact that helps explain to my American friends how I grew up eating blue marlin prepared a host of different ways. In this dish, I let the turmeric give the marlin an Indian exoticism; the Wasabi Crème Fraîche adds a kick. Best of all, the plum-wine vinaigrette rounds all the flavors out, bringing in the toasty nuttiness of the sesame oil. Hana katsuo, shaved flakes of the fish called bonito, is available in Asian markets.

SERVES 8

Turmeric-Crusted Blue Marlin

1 POUND BLUE MARLIN, CUT INTO
AN 8-INCH LOG

1 TABLESPOON SESAME OIL

1 TABLESPOON TURMERIC

Celery Root Slaw

1 CUP FISH STOCK (PAGE 12)

1 TABLESPOON SEA SALT

1 CELERY ROOT, JULIENNED

3 TABLESPOONS WASABI CRÈME FRAÎCHE
(PAGE 94)

Plum-Wine Vinaigrette

2 CUPS PLUM WINE

1 CUP DUCK STOCK (PAGE 17)

1 TABLESPOON HANA KATSUO

2 INCHES OF FRESH GINGER, SKIN ON,
CHOPPED

¼ TEASPOON CHOPPED FRESH GARLIC

1 CUP LIGHT SOY SAUCE

1 CUP SESAME OIL

EPAZOTE SPROUTS TO GARNISH

(Blue Marlin continued)

To prepare the marlin, heat a cast-iron skillet over high heat. Rub the marlin with sesame oil and lightly coat with turmeric. Sear quickly on all four sides until golden brown. Let cool, wrap tightly in plastic wrap, and refrigerate immediately to retain the cylinder shape.

To make the slaw, in a small saucepan over high heat, bring the fish stock to a rolling boil. Season the stock with sea salt. Add the celery root and cook for about 5 minutes, until al dente. Remove the celery root from the stock, drain, and cool. Combine the celery root with the Wasabi Crème Fraîche.

To prepare the vinaigrette, place all ingredients except the sesame oil in a sauté pan over high heat for approximately 20 minutes, until reduced by one third. Strain through a fine mesh strainer and let cool. Transfer to a blender and add sesame oil until emulsified.

When ready to serve, slice the chilled marlin into 24 ¼-inch-thick slices. To assemble each serving, pile about 2 tablespoons of the celery root slaw in the middle of the plate. Arrange 3 marlin slices around the slaw. Garnish the top of the slaw with epazote sprouts. Drizzle the vinaigrette around the plate and serve.

Wine notes: We turn to the Napa Valley for this one: a 1997 Caymus Conundrum, featuring both Viognier and sauvignon blanc grapes.

Truffled "Oeuf Brouillé" with Foie Gras

*H*ere is one of life's perfect little starters, the kind of snack that in my restaurant is called an *amuse bouche*, or "mouth-pleaser." Once again we're in my preferred world of truffles and foie gras, this time joining forces with scrambled eggs. This dish is meant to be very small and very elegant.

SERVES 4

4 EGGS

4 OUNCES A-GRADE FOIE GRAS

1 TABLESPOON TRUFFLE BUTTER

SALT

PEPPER

CHERVIL SPRIGS, FOR GARNISH

Prepare the eggs by cutting a 1-inch hole in the tops and removing the white and yolk. Reserve the yolks and whites for cooking. Clean the insides of the shells and set aside for presentation.

In a small sauté pan over medium heat, sear the foie gras until medium rare, approximately 20 seconds on each side. Transfer the pieces to a plate to cool, keeping the fat in the pan. Add the truffle butter to the sauté pan with the foie gras fat. Beat the egg whites and yolks together. Add to the sauté pan and scramble. Add salt and pepper to taste.

To serve, dice the foie gras and divide among the eggshells. Place each eggshell on a stand and fill with scrambled-egg mixture. Garnish each with a sprig of chervil.

Wine notes: The richness of the foie gras looks long and hard for a wine that is crisp, with a touch of toasty caramelized pear at the finish. I love a South African chardonnay called Glen Carlou, preferably the 1995 reserve.

Green Papaya au Gratin

*P*apaya trees are plentiful on the island of Mauritius. Historically, this dish was a poor man's staple, as it could be made with freely available papayas picked while still green, and day-old bread. Like so many others, this dish with its humble beginnings has been assimilated into the cuisine of the mass culture, and today is enjoyed by rich and poor alike.

SERVES 4

3 (1 ½ POUND) GREEN PAPAYAS

3 TABLESPOONS CANOLA OIL

1 ONION, DICED

3 CLOVES GARLIC, FINELY CHOPPED

½ TEASPOON CHOPPED FRESH THYME

½ TEASPOON CHOPPED FRESH PARSLEY

1 CUP WHOLE MILK

2 EGGS, WHISKED TOGETHER

4 TABLESPOONS UNSALTED BUTTER

SALT AND PEPPER

2 TABLESPOONS BREAD CRUMBS

Preheat the oven to 325°.

Peel the papayas and remove the seeds. Place in a large saucepan, cover with water, and boil until very soft. Remove and purée.

In a large sauté pan, over medium heat, heat the oil and sauté the onion, garlic, thyme, and parsley until lightly browned. Add the purée of papaya. Add the milk. Decrease the heat and cook for 3 to 4 minutes. Remove from heat and add the eggs, butter, and salt and pepper to taste. Place the mixture in a 2 quart baking or gratin dish and sprinkle breadcrumbs on top. Bake in the oven uncovered for 15 minutes, allow to cool, then serve.

SOUPS

SPLIT PEA AND APPLE-SMOKED
BACON SOUP
52

TRUFFLED LOBSTER CORN BROTH
53

SHRIMP, ARTICHOKE, AND SPINACH
SOUP
55

ROASTED EGGPLANT SOUP
57

CONCH, LOBSTER, AND WHITE BEAN
CHOWDER
58

OSTRICH CONSOMMÉ WITH TRUFFLED
FOIE GRAS POTSTICKER
60

COCONUT SHRIMP SOUP
63

GINGERED FISH BOUILLON
65

Split Pea and Apple-Smoked Bacon Soup

A terrific warming soup for the winter months, this is actually a variation on the French classic potage St. Germain. I prefer apple-smoked bacon to the traditional *lardons* because of the sweet-smoky flavor it imparts.

SERVES 8

4 CUPS SPLIT PEAS

5 CUPS WATER

2 OUNCES APPLE-SMOKED BACON, THINLY JULIENNED

¼ CUP PEELED, CHOPPED CARROTS

¼ CUP CHOPPED CELERY

¼ CUP CHOPPED SHALLOTS

¼ CUP CHOPPED LEEKS, WHITE PART ONLY

1 TEASPOON CHOPPED FRESH GARLIC

1 HAM HOCK

8 CUPS DUCK STOCK (PAGE 17)

GARLIC CROUTONS, FOR GARNISH (OPTIONAL)

Soak the split peas in the water for 1 hour, then drain. In a sauté pan over low heat, render the bacon for 5 minutes. Cool, drain into a stock pot, and chop the bacon into bits.

Heat the bacon fat and sauté the carrots, celery, shallots, leeks, and garlic for 5 minutes. Add the split peas, ham hock, and stock and bring to a boil. Decrease the heat and simmer for 30 minutes. With a slotted spoon, remove 1 cup of the cooked peas and set aside. Carefully transfer the ham hock to a cutting board. Dice the ham meat from the bone and set aside. Discard the bone.

In a blender or food processor, purée the soup until smooth. Gently return the whole peas to the soup, and stir in the bacon bits and diced ham. Garnish with garlic croutons.

Wine notes: For this dish, choose a nice white burgundy like a Chassagne Montrachet.

Truffled Lobster Corn Broth with Spaghetti of Yukon Gold and Purple Peruvian Potatoes

I have always loved corn and truffle together. To me, they are two things—like salt and pepper, or oil and vinegar—that just go well together. Meanwhile, the lobster provides its signature sweetness and the two kinds of potatoes provide texture. You'll especially like the purple color from the Peruvian variety.

SERVES 4

4 YUKON GOLD POTATOES, PEELED

4 PURPLE PERUVIAN POTATOES, PEELED

8 CUPS LOBSTER STOCK (PAGE 14)
(2 CUPS FOR BLANCHING AND 6 CUPS
FOR BROTH)

2 EARS CORN, IN HUSKS

2 TABLESPOONS DICED SHALLOTS

3 TABLESPOONS OLIVE OIL

SEA SALT

CRUSHED BLACK PEPPER

1 OUNCE TRUFFLE BUTTER

SHAVED TRUFFLES, FOR GARNISH

GOLD CORN SHOOTS, FOR GARNISH
(OPTIONAL)

(continued)

(Truffled Lobster continued)

To make the spaghetti, slice the peeled potatoes into strands using a turning slicer (also known as a Chinese slicer). In a stock pot, heat 2 cups of the stock. Add the potato strands and blanch for 2 minutes until al dente. Drain in a colander.

To make the broth, preheat a grill. Grill the corn with the husk on for 15 minutes. Remove the kernels using a sharp knife to slice along the cob. In a large sauté pan over medium heat, sauté the corn kernels and shallots for 5 minutes in olive oil. Add the remaining 6 cups of stock and bring to a boil for 5 minutes. Remove from heat and cool. Purée in a blender and strain. Place the liquid in a large sauté pan over medium heat, season with salt and pepper, and add the truffle butter.

To serve, pour the broth into individual bowls, top with the potato spaghetti, and garnish with shaved truffles and corn shoots.

Wine notes: Marsanne is a grape from the northern Rhone that is now cultivated in Switzerland and the United States. With this soup, try a Marsanne from the Carneros region of California shared by Napa and Sonoma.
Drink it young, enjoying its lightness and fruitiness.

Shrimp, Artichoke, and Spinach Soup

*I*n New Orleans, artichoke is a big favorite with the locals, who have been spoiled by finding it paired with oysters in hundreds of robust Sicilian dishes. In this soup, shrimp works even better than oysters, I think. It's important that you use only fresh spinach, because it gives the ultimate in color and taste.

SERVES 6

¼ CUP VEGETABLE OIL

5 LARGE RAW ARTICHOKE BOTTOMS, PEELED AND COARSELY CHOPPED

¼ CUP CHOPPED SHALLOTS

1 TABLESPOON CHOPPED FRESH GARLIC

¼ CUP CHOPPED CARROTS

¼ CUP CHOPPED CELERY

6 CUPS SHRIMP STOCK (PAGE 11)

1 POUND FRESH SPINACH, CLEANED

SALT

PEPPER

6 — 8 BABY ARTICHOKES

1 CUP VEGETABLE OIL

12 SMALL GRILLED SHRIMP, CUT IN HALF

18 PETIT SPINACH LEAVES

18 GREEN GARLIC SHOOTS

(continued)

Heat the oil in a large stock pot over medium heat and sauté the artichoke bottoms, shallots, garlic, carrots, and celery for 5 minutes, until lightly caramelized. Add the stock and bring to a quick boil. Simmer for 5 minutes, until everything is soft.

Add the cleaned spinach and remove from the heat. Purée in a blender until smooth, and strain through a fine sieve. Season with salt and pepper to taste.

To prepare the garnish, slice the baby artichokes into ⅛-inch slices using a Japanese mandoline. In a saucepan, heat the oil to 350° and deep-fry the artichoke slices for 10 to 15 seconds. Remove from the oil and place on towels to remove most of the oil.

To serve, pour into individual bowls and garnish each bowl with 2 or 3 baby artichoke slices, 2 pieces of shrimp, and 3 each of spinach leaves and garlic shoots.

Wine notes: As you probably know, artichoke is a dastardly thing to match wines (or wits!) with. You'll need something big, buttery, and toasty like a California chardonnay with lots of oak. Try the Patz and Hall from Napa Valley.

Roasted Eggplant Soup
with Coconut and Lemongrass

This is one of my favorite soups and one that always sells in my restaurant. It goes back to my days in California, where it seemed that anything using eggplant had a fan club. Don't overlook the duck and crab stocks, which bring rich flavor and a velvety sensation.

SERVES 8

3 WHOLE MEDIUM EGGPLANTS

3 CUPS DUCK STOCK (PAGE 17)

3 CUPS CRAB STOCK (PAGE 10)

2 TABLESPOONS CHOPPED LEMONGRASS

2 CUPS COCONUT MILK

½ CUP LIGHT SOY SAUCE

2 TABLESPOONS GINGER JUICE
(JUICER-EXTRACTED)

2 TABLESPOONS CILANTRO JUICE
(JUICER-EXTRACTED)

1 TABLESPOON JALAPEÑO JUICE
(JUICER-EXTRACTED)

½ TABLESPOON GARLIC JUICE
(JUICER-EXTRACTED)

CHOPPED CILANTRO, FOR GARNISH

COOKED FRESH CRABMEAT,
FOR GARNISH (OPTIONAL)

Preheat the oven to 350°. Arrange the eggplants in a 1-inch-deep baking pan. Bake for 20 to 25 minutes, or until soft. Cool and reserve the juice. Peel and discard skins.

Heat the stocks in a large stock pot over high heat. Add the eggplant and its juice, and lemongrass and boil for 15 minutes. Remove from the heat and purée. Strain through a fine sieve into the pot. Over low heat, add the coconut milk, soy sauce, and ginger, cilantro, jalapeño, and garlic juices. Remove from the heat and pour into bowls. Garnish with chopped cilantro and crabmeat and serve.

Wine notes: I want a Sancerre from Lucien Crochet, the perfect balance to match the creaminess and velvety texture of this soup.

Conch, Lobster, and White Bean Chowder

My twist on New England chowder draws its creaminess from white beans instead of potatoes. The conch and lobster settle in together for a memorable seafood taste. Cutting the ingredients that don't get pureéd as brunoise — julienned, then finely diced — is important for the presentation and texture of this lovely soup.

Serves 4

2 CUPS WHITE BEANS

1 POUND APPLE-SMOKED BACON

¼ CUP CHOPPED SHALLOTS

¼ CUP BRUNOISE-CUT SHALLOTS

¼ CUP CHOPPED CELERY

¼ CUP BRUNOISE-CUT CELERY

¼ CUP CHOPPED LEEKS, WHITE PART ONLY

6 CUPS CHICKEN STOCK (PAGE 17)

1 PIECE HAM HOCK

6 OUNCES CONCH

6 OUNCES SPINY LOBSTER, BRUNOISE-CUT

6 CUPS LOBSTER STOCK (PAGE 14)

SALT

PEPPER

Soak the white beans in 5 cups of water for 1 hour, then drain.

In a sauté pan over low heat, render the bacon for 5 minutes. Remove ¼ cup plus 3 tablespoons of the bacon fat from the pan. Discard the remaining fat. Transfer the bacon to a cutting board, chop into bits, and set aside for garnish.

In a stock pot, heat ¼ cup of the bacon fat, and sauté the chopped shallots, chopped celery, and the leeks for 5 minutes. Add the chicken stock, white beans, and ham hock. Bring to a quick boil over high heat. Decrease the heat and simmer for 30 minutes. Check to ensure the beans are fully cooked and tender. Remove the ham hock and discard. Purée the soup and strain through a fine sieve. Set aside.

Pound the conch flat with a mallet and chop it finely. In a sauce pot, heat the 3 tablespoons of bacon fat and sauté the conch for 4 minutes. Add the brunoise-cut celery and brunoise-cut shallots, and sauté for 3 more minutes. Add the lobster meat, lobster stock, and white bean purée. Bring to a boil. Season with salt and pepper. Serve, garnished with bacon bits.

Wine notes: I recommend a white burgundy such as a Meursault.
If you want to splurge, go with a premier cru such as Les Charmes,
Les Genevrieres, or Les Perrieres.

Ostrich Consommé
with Truffled Foie Gras Potsticker

I love just about anybody's potstickers filled with just about anything, so you can imagine how I feel about this variation, which blends two of my favorite staples: truffle and foie gras. I perfected the ostrich consommé when the legendary Jean-Louis Palladin worked with me on a special dinner in New Orleans. He taught me how to impart a hearty and velvety character to the consommé.

SERVES 6

Consommé

10 POUNDS OSTRICH NECKS, SLICED INTO 1-INCH PIECES, MEAT ON

2 CUPS CHOPPED CELERY

2 CUPS CHOPPED CARROTS

2 CUPS CHOPPED YELLOW ONION

1 BAY LEAF

2 GALLONS WATER

1 POUND DUCK GIZZARDS, CLEANED

10 EGG WHITES

2 TABLESPOONS SEA SALT

1 TABLESPOON CRACKED BLACK PEPPER

3 OSTRICH EGGSHELLS, FOR PRESENTATION

Potstickers

2 OUNCES FOIE GRAS

2 OUNCES TRUFFLE BUTTER

6 WONTON SKINS

½ OUNCE TRUFFLE, SHAVED INTO 12 THIN SLICES

1 EGG YOLK, SLIGHTLY BEATEN

To make the consommé, place the ostrich neck pieces, 1 cup each of the celery, carrots, and onion, and the bay leaf with the water in a large stock pot. Simmer over low heat for 10 hours. Check regularly to ensure that there is constant movement in the stock pot, but that it does not reach a boil. The meat must fall off the bone to absorb the richness of the stock.

Strain the stock through a cheesecloth-lined sieve. The strained liquid should be clear. Transfer to a clean stock pot and simmer until reduced to ½ gallon. Cool and refrigerate overnight. The next day the stock should appear like a gelatin. Using a spoon, remove the film of fat from the top.

Blend together the duck gizzards, egg whites, and remaining 1 cup each of celery, carrots, and onion in a food processor until puréed. Season with salt and pepper.

To clarify the consommé, combine the duck gizzard purée and consommé in a stock pot over low heat, barely simmering for 2 to 2½ hours. Check regularly to ensure that the stock does not reach a boil. The stock will form a raft (a crust of materials bound by the egg white), with the clarified consommé underneath.

Carefully break through the raft without disturbing the stock. Slowly ladle the consommé through a cheesecloth-lined sieve. The consommé must be clear, with no particles. It should be the color of a lager beer. Chill overnight.

The next day, remove any fat that may have accumulated on the top of the consommé and reheat it in a double boiler.

To prepare the ostrich eggshells, wrap a strip of scotch tape lengthwise around the empty eggshell to reinforce and prevent shattering. Using a band saw or hand saw, cut the eggshell in half through the center of the tape. Clean well and use the eggshell halves as bowls for the consommé.

To make the potstickers, sear the foie gras quickly on both sides in a hot pan, about 10 seconds on each side. Cut the foie gras into 6 pieces. Whip the truffle butter in a mixer until fluffy. Lay a wonton skin flat and place on it 1 piece of foie gras, a spoonful of truffle butter, and 2 slices of shaved truffles. Brush the edge of the wonton skin with egg yolk. Fold over diagonally into a triangle shape to form the potsticker.

(continued)

(Ostrich Consommé continued)

In boiling water, quickly blanch all 6 potstickers for 5 seconds, until soft. Allow to cool and refrigerate. When ready to serve, heat a sauté pan over medium heat and sear the potstickers on one side, for about 10 seconds. The other side remains soft.

To serve, support each eggshell within a folded cloth napkin. Pour the hot consommé into the eggshell halves and float three potstickers in each half.

Wine notes: For this dish, we look again to the graceful Loire Valley of France— spotlighting the Chinon Jeune Vigne from Joguot, bursting as it is with fruit flavors.

Coconut Shrimp Soup
with Smoked Snapper Rillette

*H*ere is a soup that's extremely complex to savor. There is layer after layer of flavor in each spoonful, with the smoked rillette adding its interest to that of the coconut milk.

SERVES 4

Soup

3 CUPS SHRIMP STOCK (PAGE 11)

1 KAFFIR LIME LEAF, FINELY CHOPPED

1 CUP COCONUT MILK

2 TABLESPOONS GINGER JUICE
(JUICER-EXTRACTED)

2 TABLESPOONS CILANTRO JUICE
(JUICER-EXTRACTED)

½ TABLESPOON GARLIC JUICE
(JUICER-EXTRACTED)

½ CUP LIGHT SOY SAUCE

1 TABLESPOON JALAPEÑO JUICE
(JUICER-EXTRACTED)

Smoked Snapper Rillette

1 (4-OUNCE) SNAPPER FILLET,
SKINNED AND BONED

1 CUP PICKLING SAUCE (PAGE 5)

4 CUPS HICKORY WOOD CHIPS
FOR SMOKING

1 CUP WATER

2 LEEK LEAVES, GREEN PARTS ONLY

(continued)

(Coconut Shrimp Soup continued)

To make the soup, in a medium stock pot, bring the shrimp stock to a boil. Add the lime leaf and continue to boil for another 5 minutes. Strain. Add the coconut milk and the remaining ingredients. Stir and simmer until ready to serve.

To make the rillette, layer the snapper fillets in a glass pan and pour the pickling juice on top. Cover with plastic wrap and refrigerate overnight, approximately 10 to 15 hours.

Put 2 cups of the wood chips in 1 cup of water and set aside to soak for 10 minutes. Place the remaining 2 cups of dry chips on the bottom of a grill or smoker. Light the chips on fire. When they are burning well, add the water-soaked chips to create smoke. Immediately place the snapper fillets over the smoke and cold-smoke them, keeping them away from the direct heat, for 15 minutes. Check every 5 minutes to ensure the fire is still burning. When cooked, remove the fillets from the fire and shred with a small fork.

To serve, blanch the leek leaves in water. Allow to cool, then cut each leaf into 2 squares. Place one quarter of the snapper rillette in the center of each square and fold over, wrapping into a small parcel. Place each snapper rillette parcel on the bottom of a soup bowl, pour hot soup over it, and serve.

Wine notes: I want something citrusy with this soup, perhaps a Sancerre from Michel Redde.

Gingered Fish Bouillon

In New Orleans everything goes into gumbo, but in Mauritius, we do bouillon, which is made without a roux so it's lighter and has layers and layers of flavor. Almost all bouillon is served over rice, either basmati or jasmine. This is my version of the one my mom used to make.

¼ CUP OLIVE OIL

2 YELLOW ONIONS, DICED

¼ CUP DICED CELERY

1 TABLESPOON DICED FENNEL

3 CLOVES GARLIC, CRUSHED

¼ CUP PEELED, DICED FRESH GINGER

10 TOMATOES, DICED

1 TEASPOON TURMERIC

1 FRESH CAYENNE PEPPER,
SEEDED AND DICED

2 POUNDS WHOLE ROUGETS,
SCALED AND GUTTED

2 POUNDS WHOLE RED SNAPPERS,
SCALED AND GUTTED

2 CUPS WHITE WINE

4 CUPS VEGETABLE STOCK (PAGE 19)

2 SPRIGS THYME

2 SPRIGS CILANTRO

1 TABLESPOON CHOPPED PARSLEY

In a large saucepan, heat the oil over medium heat and sauté the onion, celery, fennel, garlic, and ginger for 5 minutes. Add the tomato, turmeric, and cayenne. Cook for 3 minutes. Add the fish and braise for 5 minutes while turning constantly so it will absorb the liquid. Deglaze the pan with the white wine. Add the stock and thyme. Simmer for 20 minutes, making sure the fish is always covered by the liquid so it won't dry out. Do not boil. Add the cilantro and parsley just before serving.

To serve, pour over a scoop of rice on each plate. Place several fish on top.

Wine notes: Try with a sauvignon blanc from Sanford Winery in Santa Barbara.

SEAFOOD

SEARED ROUGET
ON BABY ARTICHOKE BARIGOULE
68

POMPANO ON LEMONGRASS
BRANDADE GALETTE
71

CORN-CRUSTED OPAH
AND BLUE PRAWN
74

GRILLED SCALLOPS
77

GRILLED ESCOLAR
79

LEMONGRASS-CRUSTED SKATE
81

FIRE-ROASTED SHRIMP
84

MEDALLION OF CITRUS-CURED
WILD SALMON
87

ARCTIC CHAR
89

SWEET POTATO–CRUSTED REDFISH
92

AQUAVIT-CITRUS–CURED SALMON
94

SHRIMP ROUGAIL
96

SPINY LOBSTER
98

PINE NUT–CRUSTED
SOFT-SHELL CRAB
99

Seared Rouget
on Baby Artichoke Barigoule, Haricots Verts with Saffron-Mussel Vinaigrette

*R*ouget is a delicious fish from the Mediterranean, familiar to some Americans as one of the essential ingredients in the bouillabaisse served in Marseilles. *Barigoule* is a word that's not as exotic as it sounds, describing a classic method for cooking artichokes in white wine. Rouget is quite delicate, so I go to great lengths not to overpower its special flavor, keeping the barigoule simple and also pitching the saffron-mussel vinaigrette in a way that not only pays tribute to bouillabaisse, but honors the dish's roots in Provence.

SERVES 8

Rouget Stock

2 TABLESPOONS OLIVE OIL

1 CUP CHOPPED WHITE ONION

1 CUP CHOPPED CARROTS

1 CUP CHOPPED CELERY

1 CUP CHOPPED LEEKS, BOTH WHITE AND GREEN PARTS

1 CUP WHITE WINE

3 CUPS WATER

ROUGET HEAD AND CARCASS (FROM WHOLE FISH, BELOW)

¼ CUP CHOPPED FENNEL

Baby Artichoke Barigoule

24 BABY ARTICHOKES

3 CUPS WATER

6 LEMONS AND THEIR JUICE

1 CUP PEELED, CHOPPED CARROTS

1 CUP CHOPPED CELERY

1 CUP CHOPPED SHALLOTS

5 CUPS WHITE WINE

2 TABLESPOONS CHOPPED FRESH THYME

SALT

PEPPER

Saffron-Mussel Vinaigrette

¼ CUP CHOPPED SHALLOTS

½ TEASPOON CHOPPED GARLIC

3 TABLESPOONS OLIVE OIL

1 POUND FRESH MUSSELS IN THEIR SHELLS

PINCH OF SAFFRON THREADS

½ CUP OLIVE OIL

1 TABLESPOON RICE VINEGAR

Haricots Verts

1 POUND HARICOTS VERTS, CLEANED

2 TABLESPOONS BUTTER

SALT

PEPPER

8 (4 OUNCE) WHOLE ROUGET WITH CENTRAL BONES REMOVED

To make the rouget stock, heat the oil in a large sauté pan over medium heat. Sauté the onion, carrots, celery, and leeks until lightly caramelized, about 10 minutes. Add the wine and water. Bring to a rolling boil for 3 minutes. Add the fish head and carcass and fennel. Boil for 5 minutes. Strain through a fine sieve and simmer until reduced to 1 cup of stock. Set aside. The stock will be used later in the vinaigrette.

To prepare the artichokes, peel and clean, and place them in a bowl with the water and the lemons. In a large stockpot over medium heat, sauté the carrots, celery, and shallots until lightly caramelized, approximately 5 minutes. Add the wine, thyme, and artichokes. Season with salt and pepper. Cook over low heat for 30 minutes, until the artichokes are just tender. Check for doneness with a knife, being careful not to overcook.

To prepare the vinaigrette, in a large sauté pan, cook the shallots and garlic for 3 minutes in the 3 tablespoons of olive oil. Add the mussels and rouget stock. When the mussels open, remove from the pan and set aside for garnish. Strain the stock through a fine sieve into a saucepan. Add the saffron threads and bring to a boil. Reduce to ½ cup, about 5 minutes. Transfer the stock reduction to a blender and blend in the oil and vinegar. This vinaigrette will be served warm.

(continued)

To prepare the haricots verts, blanch them in boiling water for 2 minutes. Drain. In a large sauté pan over high heat, melt the butter and sauté the haricots verts for 1 minute. Season to taste with salt and pepper.

To prepare the rouget, in a large sauté pan over medium heat, sauté the fish fillets for about 45 seconds on each side.

To assemble the individual servings, divide the haricots verts among the plates. Cut the baby artichokes in half and arrange 6 halves on each plate. Place 2 rouget fillets and 3 mussels on each plate. Drizzle with vinaigrette.

Wine notes: With this dish, I would go for a St. Joseph blanc
from Chapoutier in the Rhone Valley.

Pompano on Lemongrass Brandade Galette

with Tamarind and Coconut Relish, with Caramelized Fennel–Shrimp Broth

*F*irst off, a brandade is a traditional way the Provençals have of working with cod—in their case, nearly always the salt cod many Americans know as "bacalao." For me, salt cod is exactly that—too salty for use in my kind of food—so I make my brandade with fresh cod. I also make a galette with more delicate results by blending the cod with mashed potato. Last, but most, there's the pompano itself, the Gulf of Mexico's answer to dover sole. It's one of the world's best-tasting fish, which Mark Twain once described as equal in pleasure to the "lesser forms of sin." I'm not too sure which sins Twain had in mind, but I do love my pompano. Be sure to cook this fish with the skin on, so the meat will retain the crisp texture and light salty taste of the sea.

SERVES 4

Tamarind and Coconut Relish

2 PIECES TAMARIND, SEEDED

1 COCONUT, PEELED AND GRATED, RESERVING 1 CUP OF MILK

3 TABLESPOONS OLIVE OIL

1 TEASPOON GINGER JUICE (JUICER EXTRACTED)

1 CLOVE GARLIC, FINELY DICED

1 JALAPEÑO PEPPER, SEEDED AND JUICED

1 TEASPOON CHOPPED FRESH CILANTRO

1 TEASPOON CHOPPED FRESH MINT LEAVES

SALT

PEPPER

(continued)

(Pompano continued)

Lemongrass Brandade Galette

2 TABLESPOONS GRATED LEMONGRASS

2 CUPS WHOLE MILK

1 CUP SHRIMP STOCK (PAGE 11)

½ TEASPOON CRUSHED FRESH GARLIC

SEA SALT

BLACK PEPPER

1 POUND COD, SKINNED AND FILLETED

2 CUPS MASHED POTATOES WITHOUT THE
GARLIC (PAGE 146)

2 TABLESPOONS FINELY DICED SHALLOTS

1 CUP PANKO (JAPANESE BREADCRUMBS)

1 CUP ALL-PURPOSE FLOUR

3 EGGS, BEATEN

¼ CUP OLIVE OIL

Caramelized Fennel Sauce

1 STALK FENNEL, SLICED

2 TABLESPOONS DICED SHALLOTS

2 TABLESPOONS DICED CELERY

2 TABLESPOONS OLIVE OIL

2 CUPS RIESLING WINE

3 CUPS SHRIMP STOCK (PAGE 11)

2 TABLESPOONS BUTTER

SALT

PEPPER

2 WHOLE FRESH POMPANO,
FILLETED, SKIN ON

To make the relish, purée the tamarind with the reserved 1 cup of coconut milk, olive oil, ginger juice, and garlic and jalapeño juice in blender. Add the grated coconut, cilantro, and mint. Season with salt and pepper to taste.

To make the galettes, in a stockpot bring the lemongrass, milk, shrimp stock, and garlic to a boil for 5 minutes. Season with salt and pepper. Lower the temperature to a light simmer and add the cod to the milk. Poach the cod until medium rare, approximately 15 minutes. Remove the cod and shred in a mixing bowl. Add the mashed potatoes and shallots. Season to taste with salt and pepper.

Preheat oven to 300°. Put the panko, egg, and flour in three separate bowls. Place a ring mold on the table. Fill it ¾ of the way to the top with the brandade. Dust the molded brandade in the flour, dip it in the egg, then dust it in the panko. Sauté in olive oil over medium heat for 2 minutes on each side. Finish in the oven to make sure it is hot all the way through.

To make the sauce, sauté the fennel, shallots, and celery in olive oil for 3 minutes, until caramelized. Add the wine and boil for 3 minutes. Strain through a fine sieve. Add the shrimp stock and cook until reduced to ¼ cup, about 5 minutes and finish with butter.

To prepare the pompano, preheat the oven to 300°. Season the pompano fillets with salt and pepper. Sear, skin side first to give a nice crisp finish. Sauté on each side for 3 to 4 minutes.

To assemble each serving, place a galette on the middle of the plate. Rest a pompano fillet on the galette and top with relish. Drizzle fennel sauce around the plate.

Wine notes: How about a 1997 Matanzas Creek chardonnay with this one? The wine leads with lots of fruit and very little oak, and it has an extraordinary finish.

Corn-Crusted Opah

and Blue Prawn on Salsify and Jackfruit Salad with Watercress Vinaigrette

*W*hile you can use several types of fish with success in this presentation, I created it around the opah—an unusual fish I encountered in Hawaii on my honeymoon. Opah, which the islanders also call moonfish because of its rounded shape, actually has three different colors and three distinct textures in its flesh. It's a steak fish, and therefore should never be cooked more than medium-rare. The blue prawns from Asia contribute a very sweet and delicate taste, plus a texture similar to that of lobster. Finally, I like the combination of tropical jackfruit and salsify. Note: The jackfruit must be green for it to work right in this dish.

SERVES 6

Corn-Crusted Opah

2 CUPS AIR-DRIED CORN

6 (5-OUNCE) PIECES OPAH

SEA SALT

PEPPER

¼ CUP GRAPESEED OIL

Watercress Vinaigrette

3 CUPS SHRIMP STOCK MADE WITH BLUE PRAWN HEADS (PAGE 11)

1 CUP WATERCRESS LEAVES

½ TABLESPOON RICE VINEGAR

½ CUP GRAPESEED OIL

SEA SALT

PEPPER

Salsify and Jackfruit Salad

2 CUPS MILK

½ CUP SHRIMP STOCK
(PAGE 11) OR WATER

1 POUND SALSIFY ROOT, PEELED, CUT
INTO 24 3-INCH STICKS

2 CUPS CHICKEN STOCK
(PAGE 17) OR WATER

24 (5-INCH LONG) PIECES OF GREEN
JACKFRUIT STICKS

½ CUP GRAPESEED OIL

½ TEASPOON CRUSHED
FRESH GARLIC

SEA SALT

PEPPER

6 FLORETS WATERCRESS, FOR GARNISH

Blue Prawns

6 LARGE FRESHWATER BLUE PRAWNS,
HEADS REMOVED

SEA SALT

PEPPER

2 TABLESPOONS OLIVE OIL

To prepare the fish, crumble the corn with a roller. Season the fish with salt and pepper and crust it with the crumbled corn. In a large sauté pan over medium heat, heat the grapeseed oil and sear the fish on all sides until golden brown and medium rare, about 7 minutes. Slice each piece into 5 slices.

To prepare the vinaigrette, heat the shrimp stock in a large stockpot over high heat. Reduce to about 1 cup, approximately 10 minutes.

Bring 1 cup of the stock reduction to a simmer and add the watercress leaves. Remove from heat, purée in a blender, then strain. Add the vinegar and oil and blend. Season with salt and pepper to taste.

(continued)

To prepare the salad, bring the milk and stock to a boil. Add the salsify and decrease the heat to low. Cook for 15 to 20 minutes, until the salsify is tender. Remove the salsify and discard the liquid.

Preheat the oven to 350°. Bring the chicken stock to a boil and blanch the jackfruit in the stock for 5 minutes. The fruit will be only half cooked. Remove the jackfruit and discard the stock. Spread the grapeseed oil and garlic on a baking sheet pan and layer with the jackfruit. Bake for 5 minutes to finish.

In a mixing bowl, combine the jackfruit and salsify. Add 2 tablespoons of the vinaigrette. Season with salt and pepper to taste.

To prepare the prawns, cut them in half without cutting through the shell, butterflying the meat. Season with salt and pepper. Sauté in the oil for 1 minute on each side.

To assemble the individual servings, place 4 pieces each of the salsify and jackfruit on each plate. Garnish each with a watercress floret. Place 5 slices of opah on top of the salad. Add one blue prawn and drizzle vinaigrette around the plate.

Wine notes: I'd really like a Viognier with this, perhaps a 1997 Araujo from Napa Valley. It's quite tropical, with good acidity and a finish that always reminds me of coconut.

Grilled Scallops
with Wild Rice Galette and Red Bell Pepper Vinaigrette

I guess every chef has dishes people want him or her to keep cooking forever, and this has got to be one of mine. I love the texture of scallops even more than their light, subtle flavor—especially when they come fresh into my kitchen. I think the wild rice adds a nutty taste that works great with the sweet-tartness of the red bell pepper vinaigrette.

SERVES 4

Wild Rice Galettes

2 CUPS WILD RICE

5 CUPS WATER

10 OVEN-DRIED TOMATOES (PAGE 2)

1½ CUPS SHRIMP STOCK (PAGE 11)

½ CUP CREAM

SALT

PEPPER

1 POUND PHYLLO PASTRY

¼ CUP BUTTER, MELTED

Red Bell Pepper Vinaigrette

4 RED BELL PEPPERS, GRILLED, PEELED, AND JUICED

1 TABLESPOON RICE VINEGAR

1 CUP OLIVE OIL

SALT

PEPPER

Asparagus and Grilled Scallops

20 FRESH SCALLOPS

3 TABLESPOONS OLIVE OIL

20 ASPARAGUS SPEARS

2 TABLESPOONS BUTTER

(continued)

To prepare the galettes, in a large saucepan, cook the rice in the water until the grains are fully cooked and split open, approximately 30 minutes.

Purée the tomatoes and shrimp stock together in a blender. Strain. In a saucepan, bring the purée and cream to a boil. Add to the wild rice and mix thoroughly. Season with salt and pepper.

Preheat the oven to 350°. Brush 1 sheet of phyllo with melted butter. Repeat 3 more times, layering the sheets until you have a stack of 4 phyllo sheets. Cut the stack in half, then cut each half into 4 2-inch strips. Line a 3-inch ring mold with 4 phyllo strips in a criss-cross fashion, as illustrated on page 119. Spoon one quarter of the wild rice mixture into the mold and fold the phyllo strips over to create one galette. Remove the ring mold. Repeat this process to make 3 more galettes. Transfer the galettes to a sheet pan and bake for 8 minutes, until golden brown.

To make the vinaigrette, in a saucepan over medium heat, reduce the red pepper juice by half, about 3 minutes. Let cool and add the vinegar. Transfer to a blender and add the olive oil. Blend until the oil is fully incorporated. Season with salt and pepper to taste.

Brush the scallops with olive oil. Grill them over high heat for 1 minute on each side. Season with salt and pepper.

Cut the asparagus spears into 5-inch-long pieces. Blanch the spears, then sauté in the butter for about 1 minute. Season with salt and pepper to taste.

To assemble the individual servings, place a galette in the middle of the plate and arrange asparagus spears around it. Place 5 scallops around the outer edge of the plate and drizzle with vinaigrette.

Wine notes: This dish cries out for a bit of a splurge. Just wait until the sweet tender flesh of these grilled scallops mingles in your mouth with the bubbles of a good champagne. My recommendations include a nonvintage from Jacquesson et Fils, or the excellent 1994 Blanc de Blancs from Matanzas Creek.

Grilled Escolar
with Warm Roasted Purple Fingerling and Niçoise Olive Potato Salad, with an Apple-Smoked Bacon Vinaigrette

*E*scolar is one of the newly "discovered" fishes from the Gulf of Mexico—and newly configured for the marketplace too, because it used to be known as the far less appealing "oilfish." It is indeed rather oily, with a texture similar to white albacore tuna, except flakier. The finished dish draws just a bit of the smoke from the bacon, plus an intriguing look and flavor from the mix of purple potatoes and niçoise olives.

Serves 4

Fingerling Potatoes

15 PURPLE FINGERLING POTATOES, WHOLE

¼ CUP OVEN-DRIED TOMATO OIL (PAGE 2)

2 TABLESPOONS FINELY CHOPPED FRESH THYME

1 TABLESPOON CRUSHED, CHOPPED FRESH GARLIC

1 TABLESPOON SEA SALT

1 TABLESPOON PEPPER

Apple-Smoked Bacon Vinaigrette

1 POUND APPLE-SMOKED BACON, FINELY SLICED

4 CUPS SHRIMP STOCK (PAGE 2)

1 TABLESPOON RICE VINEGAR

¼ CUP OVEN-DRIED TOMATO OIL (PAGE 11)

SALT

PEPPER

(continued)

(Grilled Escolar continued)

Niçoise Olive Potato Salad

¼ CUP PITTED AND QUARTERED NIÇOISE OLIVES

2 TABLESPOONS FINELY DICED SHALLOTS

10 OVEN-DRIED TOMATOES (PAGE 2), FINELY DICED

1 MEDIUM HEAD FRISEE LETTUCE

Grilled Escolar

4 (8-OUNCE) PIECES FRESH ESCOLAR

¼ CUP OVEN-DRIED TOMATO OIL (PAGE 2)

BASIL SPRIGS, FOR GARNISH

CURRANT TOMATOES, FOR GARNISH

To prepare the potatoes, preheat the oven to 350°. In a stainless-steel bowl, coat the whole purple fingerlings with the Oven-Dried Tomato Oil, thyme, garlic, salt, and pepper. Bake the potatoes in a roasting pan for 20 minutes, until tender.

Meanwhile, prepare the vinaigrette. Sauté the apple-smoked bacon slices over medium heat. Cook for 15 minutes until the fat melts and the bacon is crispy. Strain and set aside the bacon for the warm salad. Cook the stock until reduced to 1 cup. Place the stock in a large mixing bowl. Add the vinegar. Whisk in the oil and the melted bacon fat. Season with salt and pepper to taste.

To assemble the salad, cut the potatoes into quarters. Place in a mixing bowl and add the olives, bacon, shallots, and Oven-Dried Tomatoes. Immediately prior to serving, add the frisee lettuce, 4 tablespoons of the vinaigrette, and toss.

To prepare the fish, heat a grill. Rub the fish with the oil. Grill the fish for 5 minutes on each side, making sure to heat it all the way through.

To assemble each individual serving, place warm potato salad on the middle of the plate. Place one piece of fish on top. Drizzle with vinaigrette. Garnish with basil sprigs and currant tomatoes.

Wine notes: Try a Muscadet with this one, perhaps the
1999 Chateau de L'Hyvernière reserve.

Lemongrass-Crusted Skate

on Spiced Jasmine Rice, Crispy Vegetables, and Spicy Crab and Coconut Nage

I love the taste of skate; it reminds me of a cross between scallop and lobster. A caution: Any skate you use must be exceedingly fresh, because it takes on an overpowering flavor otherwise. The jasmine rice I pair with this skate is essentially Indian, thanks to the garam masala I learned to love on my island of Mauritius, while the nage features many layers of flavor. The coconut milk rounds out the dish perfectly. Ketjap manis, available in Asian markets, is a thick, dark Indonesian sauce that is similar to soy but more complex.

SERVES 4

Spiced Jasmine Rice

2 CUPS JASMINE RICE

1 TEASPOON GARAM MASALA OR CURRY POWDER

1 TEASPOON GROUND TURMERIC

5½ CUPS WATER

SALT

PEPPER

Vinaigrette for Crispy Vegetables

2 TABLESPOONS SESAME OIL

1 TEASPOON LIGHT SOY SAUCE

1 TEASPOON KETJAP MANIS

(continued)

Crispy Vegetables

¼ MEDIUM SIZE DAIKON ROOT, PEELED

1 LARGE CARROT, PEELED

2 MEDIUM GREEN ZUCCHINI

2 MEDIUM YELLOW SQUASH

Spicy Crab and Coconut Nage

2 CUPS CRAB STOCK
(PAGE 10)

½ CUP COCONUT MILK

2 TABLESPOONS GINGER JUICE
(JUICER EXTRACTED)

½ TABLESPOON GARLIC JUICE
(JUICER EXTRACTED)

2 JALAPEÑO PEPPERS, SEEDED AND JUICED

2 TABLESPOONS CILANTRO JUICE

¼ CUP LIGHT SOY SAUCE

Lemongrass-Crusted Skate

4 (7-OUNCE) PIECES OF SKATE

1 STALK LEMONGRASS, FINELY GRATED

⅓ CUP ALL-PURPOSE FLOUR

2 TABLESPOONS SEA SALT

½ TABLESPOON FRESHLY CRUSHED
BLACK PEPPER

2 TABLESPOONS PEANUT OIL

To prepare the rice, in a stainless-steel mixing bowl, combine the rice, garam masala, and turmeric. Transfer to a rice cooker. Add the water, salt, and pepper. Cook for 20 minutes.

To prepare the vinaigrette, in a small stainless-steel mixing bowl combine the sesame oil, soy sauce, and ketjap manis. Set aside.

Julienne the vegetables with a Japanese mandoline, a slicer sold in cookware shops, and transfer to a mixing bowl. Add the vinaigrette and toss.

To prepare the nage, in a saucepan bring the crabstock to a boil for 2 minutes. Turn heat to low and add the coconut milk. (Note: never boil coconut milk as it will separate.) Add the rest of the ingredients, and remove from heat. Set aside.

To prepare the skate, clean it and slice into a fan. Mix the grated lemongrass, flour, sea salt, and pepper together. Crust the skate with the lemongrass mixture. Add the peanut oil to a sauté pan and heat on a high flame. Cook the skate for 3 minutes on each side, until golden brown.

To assemble each individual serving, fill a 6-ounce ramekin with rice. Invert the ramekin onto the center of the plate. Drizzle nage around the rice. Place one portion of skate on top of the rice and top with crispy vegetables.

Wine notes: Try the great 1997 Gewürztraminer
from Gundlach Bundschu in Sonoma.

Fire-Roasted Shrimp

with Toasted Peanut Orzo and Kaffir-Lime–Ginger Fumet with Crunchy Vegetables

*H*ere is one of my all-time favorite dishes built around shrimp. It draws its heat from the Scotch bonnet peppers, an irregularly shaped chile favored in the Caribbean that is closely related to the habanero, and a bit of sweet from its flirtation with Asian ingredients for the orzo. I particularly like what happens when you mix garam masala—the real Indian version of what we call curry powder—with the kaffir lime leaf and ginger broth.

SERVES 4

Chile Oil

1 BUNCH CILANTRO

1 LARGE SHALLOT

1 2-INCH PIECE OF PEELED, FRESH GINGER

½ CUP CANOLA OIL

¼ CUP SESAME OIL (NOT TOASTED)

3 SEEDED SCOTCH BONNET PEPPERS

Fire-Roasted Shrimp with Toasted Peanut Orzo and Kaffir-Lime–Ginger Fumet

1 POUND SHRIMP (JUMBO)

2 TEASPOONS CHILE OIL (SEE ABOVE)

1 TEASPOON SEA SALT

2 TABLESPOONS COCONUT MILK

1 TABLESPOON LIGHT SOY SAUCE

2 TABLESPOONS GINGER JUICE (JUICER EXTRACTED)

1 TEASPOON CANOLA OIL

1 SMALL CARROT, CHOPPED

1 STALK CELERY, CHOPPED

2 CUPS WATER

2 CLOVES GARLIC, CHOPPED

2 KAFFIR LIME LEAVES, JULIENNED

½ TEASPOON GARAM MASALA OR
CURRY POWDER

1½ CUPS DRY ORZO PASTA

½ CUP CRUSHED PEANUTS

¼ CUP PEANUT OIL

Crunchy Vegetables

½ TEASPOON SALT

1 TABLESPOON FRESHLY SQUEEZED
LIME JUICE

1 TEASPOON CHILE OIL

1 TEASPOON SUGAR

2 CUPS JULIENNED MIXED VEGETABLES,
SUCH AS CARROTS, DAIKON, JICAMA,
ZUCCHINI, SQUASH

SALT

PEPPER

To make the chile oil, cut off the cilantro stems and set aside the leafy portion. Put the stems in a small nonreactive saucepan. Trim and chop the shallot and set aside the chopped shallot. Add the trimmings to the cilantro stems. Finely grate the ginger and place it in a square of cheesecloth. Twist to squeeze the ginger juice into the liquid in another pan. Set aside the pan of juice. Add the pulp to the stems and trimmings.

Add the canola oil, sesame oil, and chiles to the pan of stems, trimmings, and pulp. Bring to a boil over medium heat. Remove from the heat and let cool to room temperature. Strain through a fine sieve into a small container; discard solids. Yields about ⅔ cup. (The oil will keep, covered, in the refrigerator for up to 2 weeks.)

To prepare the shrimp and orzo, boil a large pot of salted water for cooking the orzo. Peel and devein the shrimp, leaving the tails intact. Reserve the shells and heads. Chop enough of the reserved leafy portion of the cilantro to yield 6 tablespoons. In a bowl, combine 2 tablespoons of the cilantro, the chile oil, and sea salt. Add the shrimp and toss to coat. Cover and set aside in the refrigerator.

Add the coconut milk and soy sauce to the ginger juice and set aside.

(continued)

In a saucepan, heat the canola oil over medium heat. Add the carrots, celery, and reserved chopped shallots. Cook about 3 minutes, until softened. Add the water and bring to a boil. Add the reserved shrimp shells and heads, garlic, kaffir lime leaves, and garam masala. Decrease the heat to low and simmer uncovered for 20 minutes. Transfer the shrimp-shell mixture to a blender or food processor and process until the shells are finely chopped. Strain and press through a fine sieve into a small saucepan. Retain the broth in the saucepan, discarding the solids.

Cook the orzo pasta in boiling water until al dente, 7 to 8 minutes. Drain. Heat the peanut oil and sauté the crushed peanuts. Add to the orzo pasta. Mix in the ginger/coconut milk sauce and the chopped cilantro leaves from the chili oil.

Meanwhile, heat a large heavy skillet over high heat. Add the reserved marinated shrimp and sauté until they are opaque in the center, about 4 minutes.

To make the crunchy vegetables, in a medium bowl, whisk together the salt, lime juice, chile oil, and sugar. Add the vegetables and toss to coat. Season with pepper and additional salt to taste. (The vegetables will keep, covered, in the refrigerator for up to 1 hour. They are also delicious in a light salad.)

To serve, reheat the coconut broth without boiling, if necessary, and add the remaining 3 tablespoons of cilantro. Mound orzo pasta in the center of each plate and pool shrimp broth around it. Arrange the shrimp over the broth. Garnish with crunchy vegetables.

Serving note: You can use a small ring mold to form the orzo into a cylinder in the center of each dinner plate. (You can improvise by using a clean 8-ounce can with both top and bottom removed.) Lightly oil the mold and center it on the plate. Spoon the orzo into the mold, press down firmly to pack it full, then carefully lift the mold.

Wine notes: Check out the Cloudy Bay sauvignon blanc from New Zealand.

Medallion of Citrus-Crusted Wild Salmon with Napa Cabbage Slaw and Chinese Mustard-Soy Vinaigrette

I created this dish around the spectacular salmon from the Columbia River, which I tasted during a stint as a guest chef in Seattle. Encountering its redder-than-usual flesh and its unique flavor set me on the right road. Of course, made properly, this salmon must be served rare, or at most medium-rare.

SERVES 4

Citrus-Crusted Wild Salmon

2 (1-POUND) WILD SALMON FILLETS

2 LEMONS, ZESTED

2 LIMES, ZESTED

2 ORANGES, ZESTED

4 TEASPOONS CHOPPED FRESH THYME

4 TEASPOONS CHOPPED FRESH ROSEMARY

2 TEASPOONS SEA SALT

2 TEASPOONS SESAME OIL

Chinese Mustard and Soy Vinaigrette

½ CUP SOY SAUCE

2 TABLESPOONS MOLASSES

1 TEASPOON CHINESE MUSTARD

1 TEASPOON HABANERO VINEGAR (PAGE 4)

½ CUP SESAME OIL

½ CUP GRAPESEED OIL

(continued)

Napa Cabbage Slaw

¼ CUP SHIITAKE

¼ HEAD NAPA CABBAGE

¼ RED BELL PEPPER

¼ YELLOW BELL PEPPER

¼ GREEN BELL PEPPER

¼ CUP RED ONION

PETITE LETTUCE, FOR GARNISH

PETITE BOK CHOY, FOR GARNISH

To prepare the salmon, cut the fillet in half, lengthwise. Combine the lemon, lime, and orange zests with the thyme, rosemary, and salt. Brush the salmon with sesame oil and crust it with the zest-herb mixture. In a sauté pan over high heat, quickly sear the salmon on both sides to medium rare. Wrap tightly in plastic wrap and chill. Slice into 20 ½-inch-thick medallions.

To prepare the vinaigrette, whisk all the ingredients together in a stainless-steel mixing bowl.

To prepare the slaw, slice the shiitake and finely julienne all the other vegetables. Combine all ingredients in a stainless-steel mixing bowl. Add ¼ cup of the vinaigrette and mix just before serving.

To serve, place a small ring mold in the center of an individual plate and fill it with the slaw. Arrange five medallions of the salmon around the slaw in a pinwheel and drizzle with the remaining vinaigrette. Serve immediately.

Wine notes: For its high acidity and delightful complexity,
I enjoy this dish with a Vouvray from the Loire Valley.
Make sure you get a crisp dry white with its remarkable
honey citrus flavor, not a sweet Vouvray.

Arctic Char
on Celery Root
and Lobster Mushroom with
Manila Clamand Asparagus Essence

I like to use farm-raised char because of its delicate flavor, a cross between trout and salmon. This is such a great fish that, in fact, I don't believe in doing much to it. The Manila clams are about the same size as those from the coast of the United States; I simply like the taste better. The lobster mushroom got its name from the way it turns red when sautéed.

SERVES 6

Arctic Char

6 (5-OUNCE) PORTIONS OF ARCTIC CHAR, SKIN ON, PIN BONE OUT

¼ CUP OLIVE OIL

1 TABLESPOON CHOPPED FRESH GARLIC

(continued)

Celery Root

2 WHOLE CELERY ROOT, PEELED, CUT
INTO 1-INCH SLICES AND DICED

¼ CUP OLIVE OIL

1 TEASPOON FINELY CHOPPED FRESH
GARLIC

¼ CUP FINELY CHOPPED SHALLOTS

1 POUND CLEANED AND DICED LOBSTER
MUSHROOMS

SEA SALT

PEPPER

Manila Clam and Asparagus Essence

36 ASPARAGUS STALKS

2 TABLESPOONS OLIVE OIL

30 CLAMS, FRESH WITH SHELLS CLOSED

1 CUP FISH FUMET (PAGE 13)

¼ CUP FINELY CHOPPED FRESH SHALLOTS

2 TABLESPOONS BUTTER

4 CUPS WATER

SALT

PEPPER

To prepare the fish, rub it with the olive oil and garlic. In a large pan over medium heat, sauté the fish on the skin side first for 3 minutes, then on the other side for 3 minutes, until cooked medium-rare.

To prepare the celery root, in a large sauté pan over high heat, sauté the celery root in the oil until crispy, approximately 7 minutes. Add the garlic, shallots, and mushrooms. Sauté for 5 minutes and season with salt and pepper.

To prepare the essence, brush half of the asparagus stalks with 1 tablespoon of the olive oil and grill for 2 minutes. Juice the asparagus stalks in a juicer and set aside.

In a large stockpot, steam the clams with the fish fumet and shallots until the clams open, approximately 7 minutes on medium heat. Transfer the juice from the clams to a small saucepan. Add the asparagus juice. Reduce to 1 cup on low heat, approximately 10 minutes. Whisk in 1 tablespoon of the butter and season with salt and pepper to make a sauce.

Cut off the stems—the tougher, more fibrous ends—of the remaining asparagus stalks, leaving 3-inch tip sections. Blanch the tips in 4 cups of boiling water. Drain. In a saucepan, combine the remaining 1 tablespoon of butter with 1 tablespoon olive oil and sauté the asparagus tips for 1 minute. Season to taste with salt and pepper.

To assemble each individual serving, place celery root–mushroom mixture on the center of the plate. Top with 1 portion of fish, 5 clams, and 3 asparagus tips. Drizzle with the clam-asparagus essence.

Wine notes: The flavors here are perfectly spotlighted by a complex white burgundy, such as a Chassagne Montrachet.

Sweet Potato–Crusted Redfish
with Kumquat Beurre Blanc

*T*hanks to Cajun cooking, most of the world knows about Louisiana redfish—the fish driven toward extinction by the craze for blackening. After a lot of protection, the population is strong again. And I think this is one of the best ways to enjoy the meat's terrific flavor, without the cover-up provided by heavy-handed Cajun spices. Kumquats, by the way, are a favored south Louisiana citrus crop, hailing from Plaquemines Parish along the Mississippi River.

SERVES 8

8 SWEET POTATOES, PEELED

OIL FOR DEEP-FRYING

Kumquat Beurre Blanc

1 TABLESPOON OLIVE OIL

3 SHALLOTS, DICED

1 POUND KUMQUATS, CHOPPED WITH SKIN ON

1 CUP DRY VERMOUTH

½ CUP (1 STICK) UNSALTED BUTTER

Redfish

8 (6- TO 8-OUNCE) REDFISH OR RED SNAPPER FILLETS

4 TABLESPOONS OLIVE OIL

SALT

FRESHLY GROUND BLACK PEPPER

SLICED KUMQUATS, FOR GARNISH (OPTIONAL)

Slice the sweet potatoes lengthwise into ¼-inch-thick slices. Cover with cold water and soak for about 20 minutes to remove the natural sugar.

To prepare the beurre blanc, heat the oil in a small saucepan over medium-high heat. Add the shallots and kumquats and sauté until soft, about 5 minutes. Deglaze the pan with the vermouth, scraping up the brown particles from the bottom. Boil to reduce the liquid by half, then stir in the butter until the sauce is thickened and shimmering.

To prepare the sweet potatoes, preheat the deep-frying oil to 375°. Dry the potato slices thoroughly, then deep-fry until they are crispy. Set aside a few of the potato chips to use as a garnish, if desired. Process the remaining fried potatoes with the chopping blade of a food processor until they look like cornflakes.

To prepare the fish, preheat the oven to 350°. Brush the redfish with the oil and season with salt and pepper. Sprinkle the fish with the potato flakes, then sear in a frying pan, about 1 minute on each side. To finish, bake the fish in the oven for 5 minutes.

To serve, arrange the redfish fillets on dinner plates and spoon the sauce around the sides. Garnish with additional kumquat slices and sweet potato chips, if desired.

Wine notes: To slice right through the sweetness of the sauce and the crustiness of the fish, I like a Cakebread chardonnay from Napa.

Aquavit-Citrus–Cured Salmon
with Osetra Caviar and Wasabi Crème Fraîche

The dish gives us salmon that is cured in aquavit, a vodka flavored with caraway seeds. The fish is formed by pressing into a ring mold with wasabi crème fraîche, which gives the whole affair a pleasant pungency. The caviar on top provides the saltiness I think the dish needs. Note: The salmon must cure for 72 hours before assembling the dish.

SERVES 8

Salmon

2 SALMON FILLETS (ABOUT 3 POUNDS TOTAL)

ZEST OF 10 LIMES

ZEST OF 10 ORANGES

ZEST OF 10 LEMONS

1 CUP SEA-SALT CRYSTALS

3 CUPS GRANULATED SUGAR

1 750-ML BOTTLE AQUAVIT

Wasabi Crème Fraîche

1 CUP CRÈME FRAÎCHE (PAGE 3)

1 TEASPOON WASABI PASTE

4 OUNCES OSETRA CAVIAR

1 CUP DILL SPRIGS, FOR GARNISH

To prepare the salmon, place the fillets in a large glass baking dish. Combine the citrus zests, salt, sugar, and aquavit in a large stainless-steel mixing bowl. Pour the mixture over the salmon and cover tightly with plastic wrap. Refrigerate for 72 hours to cure.

Prepare the crème fraîche. Fold the wasabi paste into the crème fraîche until it is fully incorporated and smooth.

To serve, dice the cured salmon into ⅛ inch cubes. Fold the salmon into the crème fraîche. Center a large ring mold on a dinner plate and fill to the top with the salmon mixture. Spread about 1 teaspoon of caviar on top in a thin, even layer. Remove the ring mold and garnish with dill. Serve immediately.

Wine notes: For its intense fruit aftertaste, I recommend a sauvignon blanc like the Brancott "B" from New Zealand. It will really cleanse your palate, whisking away the saltiness of the caviar.

Shrimp Rougail
with Mango Chutney

*R*ougail is a Mauritian classic, kind of like marinara for the Italians. You can use this same sauce with many different dishes, but my favorite is with shrimp. There is no set way to do rougail, so once you've made it a few times, play around with the ingredients to suit your taste. Every Mauritian family, whether Indian, Chinese, Creole, or European, cooks rougail about once a week. The secret is to make sure the tomatoes are ripe. When you serve it with this mango chutney, you'll almost feel the tropical breeze on your skin. Using a mortar and pestle is still very common in Mauritius. Often a wooden block and a large wine bottle will be used to crush the spices.

SERVES 6 TO 8

Mango Chutney

2 POUNDS GREEN MANGO

1 1-INCH-LONG PIECE PEELED FRESH GINGER

2 CLOVES GARLIC

2 YELLOW ONIONS, FINELY DICED

1 TEASPOON CRUSHED, DICED, AND

SEEDED HOT GREEN PEPPERS

3 TABLESPOONS OLIVE OIL

PINCH OF TURMERIC

1 TABLESPOON WHITE WINE VINEGAR

SALT

PEPPER

Shrimp Rougail

20 RIPE ROMA TOMATOES

¼ CUP OLIVE OIL

2 YELLOW ONIONS, DICED

6 CLOVES GARLIC, CRUSHED

1 2-INCH-LONG PIECE PEELED FRESH
GINGER, FINELY DICED

½ TEASPOON TURMERIC

½ TEASPOON GARAM MASALA

OR CURRY POWDER

4 CURRY LEAVES

2 TABLESPOONS CHOPPED FRESH PARSLEY

2 TABLESPOONS CHOPPED FRESH THYME

2 POUNDS UNCOOKED PEELED MEDIUM
SHRIMP

SALT

PEPPER

To make the mango chutney, grate the mango and set aside. Crush the ginger, garlic, onions, and peppers with a mortar and pestle. Heat the oil in a pan over medium heat. Sauté the pepper paste with the turmeric for 2 minutes. Remove from heat. Deglaze the pan with the vinegar. Allow to cool. Place in a mixing bowl, add the mango, and mix well. Add salt and pepper to taste.

To make the rougail, grill the tomatoes over a medium flame for 5 minutes. Allow to cool. Peel and purée in a blender until smooth. Set aside.

In large sauté pan, heat the oil. Sauté the onion in the oil for 2 minutes. Add the garlic and ginger and sauté for 3 minutes. Add the turmeric and garam masala and cook for 3 minutes. Add the tomato purée and curry leaves and cook for 5 minutes. Add the shrimp and cook for 5 minutes. Add the parsley and thyme and season with salt and pepper.

Serve over basmati or jasmine white rice with the mango chutney on the side.

Wine notes: Try this dish with a Bandol rosé from Provence.

Spiny Lobster
with Pineapple Sauce

This dish is a wonderfully tasty example of the fusion of cultural cooking which often manifests in Mauritius due to the diverse population. It originated with the Creoles in Mauritius: they used lobster caught in the Indian Ocean, dicing it with pineapple and onions, and grilling it. Later, the French added classic components to form the sauce which complements the dish.

SERVES 4

4 (1 POUND) SPINY LOBSTER TAILS

2 TABLESPOONS CANOLA OIL

1 LARGE ONION, DICED

2 SHALLOTS, DICED

3 CLOVES GARLIC, CHOPPED

1 PINEAPPLE, HALF DICED AND HALF JUICED

1 CUP VERMOUTH

6 TABLESPOONS UNSALTED BUTTER

1 CUP CRÈME FRAÎCHE (PAGE 3)

Place the lobsters in a large pot with water and boil for about 5 minutes. Remove and allow to cool. Peel the tails and cut into medallions 1 inch thick.

In a large pan, heat the oil over medium heat. Add the onion, shallots and garlic. Sauté until lightly browned. Add the lobster tails and diced pineapple. Cook the lobster halfway and remove from pan and set aside in a separate bowl. Add vermouth and pineapple juice to the pan and cook until reduced to a third. Whisk in butter to make a beurre blanc. Add the crème fraîche and lobster tails and simmer for approximately 2 minutes.

To serve, pile the medallions in the center of each plate. Pour the sauce on top.

Wine notes: I'd recommend the Chablis Domaine Laroche. It will cut right through the butter and cream, cleaning your palate between bites.

Pine Nut–Crusted Soft-Shell Crab
with Celery-Root Tempura and Lemon-Preserve Vinaigrette

*T*hough other places around the country share New Orleans' love of soft-shell crabs, it's here that I learned to appreciate their special charms. Essentially, they are crabs harvested after outgrowing their old hard shell—before they can produce a new one. Instead of the frying so popular locally, I sauté my soft-shell crabs. As a planning note, it's best if you make the lemon preserve about two weeks in advance.

SERVES 4

Lemon Preserve

5 LEMONS, SPIKED ALL OVER WITH A FORK

2 CUPS WHITE WINE

¾ CUP SUGAR

¼ CUP SEA SALT

5 SPRIGS THYME

5 SPRIGS TARRAGON

5 SPRIGS BASIL

Pine nut–Crusted Soft-shell Crab

½ CUP PINE NUTS, TOASTED

2 TABLESPOONS ALL-PURPOSE FLOUR

1 TABLESPOON SEA SALT

½ TABLESPOON BLACK PEPPER

4 WHOLE SOFT-SHELL CRABS

2 TABLESPOONS OLIVE OIL

(continued)

Vinaigrette

½ PRESERVED LEMON, SEEDED
(RECIPE ABOVE)

3 TABLESPOONS WINE FROM THE LEMON
PRESERVES (RECIPE ABOVE)

1 JALAPEÑO PEPPER, SEEDED AND JUICED
IN A JUICER

1 CUP OLIVE OIL

SALT

PEPPER

Celery-Root Tempura

¾ CUP ALL-PURPOSE FLOUR

¼ CUP CORNSTARCH

½ TEASPOON SUGAR

½ TEASPOON SALT

2 CUPS LIGHT BEER

1 CELERY ROOT

3 CUPS OLIVE OIL, FOR DEEP-FRYING

SALT

To make the preserve, in a saucepan on low heat, combine the lemons, wine, sugar, salt, thyme, tarragon, and basil. Simmer for 1½ to 2 hours (the lemons should be soft). Cool and refrigerate in a lidded jar for 2 weeks to preserve.

To prepare the crabs, preheat the oven to 350°. Crush the toasted pine nuts into a powder with a rolling pin. Transfer to a mixing bowl and stir in the flour, salt, and pepper. Dredge the soft-shell crab in the coating mixture. Heat the olive oil in a large sauté pan and sauté the crabs for 2 minutes on each side. Finish by baking for 3 minutes just before serving.

To prepare the vinaigrette, purée the lemon, wine, and jalapeño juice together. Add the olive oil and season with salt and pepper to taste.

To prepare the tempura, mix together the flour, cornstarch, sugar, and salt. Add the beer and mix to make a smooth batter. Let stand for 20 minutes.

Slice the celery root into 4 (¾-inch) slices. Blanch in boiling water for 2 minutes. Let cool and pat dry. Heat the oil to 375°. Season the celery-root slices with salt and pepper and coat in the tempura batter. Deep-fry for 1 minute. Remove from the oil with a slotted spoon and drain on paper towels.

To serve, place the celery root slices on the center of a platter and top with the soft-shell crabs. Drizzle with vinaigrette. Serve the chutney on the side.

Wine notes: I actually prefer beer instead of wine with this dish, at least to accentuate the beer batter. The New Orleans area is lucky to have a local beer from Abita Springs. One of the lighter brews would work best with this dish.

POULTRY

Cassoulet of Seared Hudson Valley Duck Breast, Foie Gras, Duck Confit, and Merguez Sausage on Flageolet Beans

Like most people, I love the cassoulet served in and around Toulouse, but I like to adjust the recipe a bit more than the next chef. I substitute slightly spicy Moroccan merguez for the sausage of Toulouse, and I find flageolet beans creamier than the plain white beans used in the original.

SERVES 4

Cassoulet

2 CUPS FLAGEOLET BEANS

6 CUPS DUCK STOCK (PAGE 17)

2 HAM HOCKS

4 LINKS MERGUEZ SAUSAGE (PAGE 129), OR OTHER SPICY LINK SAUSAGE

2 (12-OUNCE) DUCK BREASTS, PREFERABLY FROM THE HUDSON VALLEY

Foie Gras

4 (1-OUNCE) PORTIONS FOIE GRAS

SEA SALT

FRESHLY CRUSHED BLACK PEPPER

Sauce

¼ CUP APPLE-SMOKED BACON, SLICED

¼ CUP CHOPPED SHALLOTS

¼ CUP MERLOT WINE

4 CUPS DUCK STOCK (PAGE 17), REDUCED BY HALF

¼ CUP OVEN-DRIED TOMATOES (PAGE 2), DICED

2 LEGS OF DUCK CONFIT (PAGE 6), SHREDDED

FRESH THYME, FOR GARNISH

To make the cassoulet, soak the beans in 4 cups of water for 1 hour, then drain. In a large stockpot over medium heat, combine the stock, ham hocks, and beans. Bring to a slow boil for 35 minutes, until the beans are cooked. Transfer the beans to another pot and allow to cool. Transfer the ham hocks to a cutting board, remove the skin and discard, and cut up the meat brunoise, julienned then finely diced. Add the meat to the beans.

Add the duck stock to the cassoulet.

Grill the sausages on a preheated grill for 5 to 7 minutes over medium heat.

Preheat the oven to 300°. In a sauté pan over medium heat, sauté the duck breasts without oil, fat side down. Drain off the rendered fat and continue cooking the breasts until golden brown, approximately 4 minutes. Turn the breasts meat side down and cook about 10 minutes more, until rare. Finish by baking for 15 minutes. Remove from the oven and let rest for 5 minutes. Slice the meat and set aside.

To prepare the foie gras, season it with salt and pepper. In a medium-size sauté pan over medium heat, sauté for 30 seconds on each side.

To prepare the sauce, in a saucepan over medium heat, cook the bacon about 5 minutes, then drain off and discard about three quarters of the rendered fat. Add the shallots to the pan and sauté for 2 minutes. Deglaze the pan with the wine and reduce the liquid for about 5 minutes, until syrupy. Add the reduced stock, or demiglace, and combine thoroughly.

To finish the bean cassoulet, add the tomatoes, ½ cup of the sauce, and the shredded confit. Mix well and heat thoroughly.

To serve, in individual bowls place the bean cassoulet in the middle and arrange a border of duck breast slices around the beans. Center the foie gras and merguez sausage on the beans. Drizzle with sauce and garnish with fresh thyme.

Wine notes: You can't beat a good Bordeaux with this cassoulet. My suggestions include Chateau Talbot and Chateau Duhart-Milon-Rothschild.

Grilled Sesame-Crusted Chicken with Baby Bok Choy and Hoisin-Ginger Vinaigrette

*T*his is my take on a California-style main course salad with crunchy Asian vegetables. I was pressed to come up with this as a lunch entrée for the well-heeled, health-conscious patrons of the Beverly Hills restaurant where I did a stint before taking up residence in New Orleans. This dish came with me, and it's so good that even New Orleanians — who care little for things that seem too low-cal or healthy — clamor for it at Dominique's.

SERVES 8

Vinaigrette

½ CUP LIGHT SOY SAUCE

½ CUP HOISIN SAUCE

1 CUP SESAME OIL

1 CUP PEANUT OIL

¼ CUP HONEY

1 3-INCH-LONG PIECE PEELED FRESH GINGER

2 TABLESPOONS RICE VINEGAR

4 CLOVES GARLIC, PEELED

2 JALAPEÑO PEPPERS, SEEDED AND JULIENNED

1 CUP CHOPPED FRESH CILANTRO

Chicken

8 (8-OUNCE) DOUBLE CHICKEN BREASTS, SKINNED

¼ CUP WHITE SESAME SEEDS

¼ CUP BLACK SESAME SEEDS

Bok Choy

8 BABY BOK CHOY, JULIENNED

1 RED BELL PEPPER, JULIENNED

1 YELLOW BELL PEPPER, JULIENNED

1 GREEN BELL PEPPER, JULIENNED

1 POUND SHIITAKE MUSHROOMS, STEMMED AND JULIENNED

CELLOPHANE NOODLES, FOR GARNISH (OPTIONAL)

To make the vinaigrette, mix all the ingredients in a blender until emulsified.

Marinate the chicken in 1 cup of the vinaigrette for 30 minutes. Remove the chicken from the vinaigrette, combine the sesame seeds and sprinkle over the chicken. Grill the chicken over a grill preheated to medium heat for 4 minutes on each side.

To make the bok choy, combine all the ingredients in a large mixing bowl. Add 1 cup of the vinaigrette and mix well.

Deep-fry the cellophane noodles for 5 seconds in peanut oil preheated to 350°, until puffed up. Drain on a towel, then break into small pieces.

To serve, place the bok choy in the center of each dinner plate. Slice the chicken breasts lengthwise and arrange around the bok choy. Drizzle with additional vinaigrette and scatter with noodles cut into small pieces for garnish.

Wine notes: A 1995 Mercurey Flaiveley Clos Rochette would
really set this dish off to its best advantage.

Mousseline of
Free-Range Chicken
with Goat Cheese–Niçoise Olive Tapenade, Roasted Tomato, and Eight-Year-Old Balsamic Vinegar

*H*ere is my spin on the continental classic I cooked years ago in London. I love the way the chicken and goat cheese come together in this super-smooth mousseline. The sweetness of the oven-dried tomatoes kicks in then, as does a special tartness from the balsamic vinegar.

SERVES 4

Mousseline

3 (6-OUNCE) FREE-RANGE CHICKEN BREASTS, SKINLESS

4 CUPS CHICKEN STOCK (PAGE 17), REDUCED BY ONE THIRD

1 EGG YOLK

3 EGG WHITES

2 OUNCES GOAT CHEESE

1 CUP HEAVY CREAM

KOSHER OR TABLE SALT

PEPPER

2 TABLESPOONS UNSALTED BUTTER

Tapenade

½ CUP PITTED NIÇOISE OLIVES

4 BASIL LEAVES

½ TEASPOON MINCED FRESH GARLIC

¼ CUP TUSCAN OLIVE OIL

4 OVEN-DRIED TOMATOES (PAGE 2), DICED

4 TABLESPOONS 8-YEAR-OLD BALSAMIC VINEGAR

To prepare the mousseline, clean the uncooked chicken breasts, carefully removing all veins. Dice into 1-inch cubes. Transfer the diced chicken to a food processor and purée until smooth, about 1 minute. Do not overwork the meat. Add the chicken stock, egg yolk, and egg whites. Purée again. Strain the mixture through a fine sieve into a large mixing bowl. Discard fibers and sinews. Refrigerate the purée immediately, then clean the food processor. Transfer the purée back to the clean food processor, then add the goat cheese and heavy cream. Blend quickly. Season with salt and pepper and refrigerate immediately until you are ready to bake.

Preheat the oven to 300°. Brush 4 4-ounce ramekins with butter. Divide the refrigerated mixture into the four ramekins and place them in a water bath. Cover with aluminum foil and bake for 20 minutes, until the mixture is set.

To make the tapenade, blend the olives in a food processor for approximately 30 seconds, until the mixture reaches a coarsely chopped consistency. Add the basil leaves and garlic. Continue to pulse until fully incorporated. Slowly add while running the blender on low the Tuscan olive oil until the tapenade is smooth. Refrigerate.

To serve, loosen the baked mousselines by running the tip of a sharp knife around the edge of the ramekins. Invert each onto the center of a dinner plate. Surround each mousseline with tapenade and sprinkle the edge of the plate with diced oven-dried tomatoes. Drizzle the outer edge of the plate with the vinegar.

Wine notes: To me, this dish cries out for a white burgundy.
For instance, St. Aubin from Verget.

Lavender-Smoked Goose Breast
on a Fig and White Corn Pain Perdu
with Apple-Merlot Reduction

*A*lthough lavender is one of the defining flavors of Provence, I came up with this dish to honor my friends at Matanzas Creek Winery in Sonoma. In addition to their terrific grapes, Matanzas grows loads of lavender on their vineyard property. (You can purchase lavender pods and wood from them. Call 800-590-6464.) To smoke the goose, I keep the faith, using wood chips from Matanzas Creek merlot barrels. The whole idea is to bring out the natural sweetness of the goose breast, set as it is against a delicious fig and corn *pain perdu*. Around New Orleans, most people know what *pain perdu* means—"lost bread" is an old Creole way of using up day-old bread. It's usually an upgraded version of what America likes to call French toast. Of course, it isn't usually made with figs and corn.

SERVES 4

Goose

1 TABLESPOON PALM SUGAR

2 CUPS MERLOT WINE

1 TABLESPOON LAVENDER PODS

1 TABLESPOON CHOPPED THYME

1 TABLESPOON SEA SALT

¼ CUP GRAPESEED OIL

1 (12- TO 14-OUNCE) GOOSE BREAST, WITH 75% OF FAT REMOVED

2 GOOSE LEGS

2 CUPS RENDERED GOOSE FAT

2 CUPS GOOSE CONFIT (FOLLOW RECIPE FOR DUCK CONFIT (PAGE 6) USING GOOSE LEGS AND GOOSE FAT INSTEAD OF DUCK LEGS AND DUCK FAT)

6 CUPS MERLOT CHIPS AND LAVENDER WOOD, FOR SMOKING

Brioche

4 CUPS BREAD FLOUR

2 TABLESPOONS DRY YEAST

2 TABLESPOONS SALT

1⅓ CUPS BUTTER

3 TABLESPOONS SUGAR

5 EGGS

½ CUP WARM WATER

Fig and White Corn Pain Perdu

1 EAR WHITE CORN, HUSK REMOVED

½ CUP (ABOUT 6) PRESERVED MISSION FIGS, DICED

2 EGGS, BEATEN

1 CUP CREAM

½ CUP MILK

SALT

PEPPER

1 TEASPOON BUTTER

Apple-Merlot Reduction

3 TABLESPOONS GOOSE FAT

½ CUP FINELY CHOPPED CELERY

½ CUP FINELY CHOPPED CARROTS

½ CUP FINELY CHOPPED ONION

1 APPLE, CORED AND CHOPPED

1 CUP MERLOT WINE

4 CUPS DUCK STOCK (PAGE 17)

SALT

PEPPER

2 OUNCES FOIE GRAS, CHILLED AND FINELY DICED

FRESH LAVENDER FLOWERS, FOR GARNISH

(continued)

To prepare the goose, melt the sugar into a syrup. Puree 1 cup of the red wine with the lavender pod, thyme, sugar syrup, salt, and grapeseed oil in a blender. Place the goose breast in a roasting pan. Pour the puréed mixture over the goose breast and marinate in the refrigerator overnight, 12 hours. The following day, soak 3 cups of the merlot chips and lavender wood in the other cup of red wine.

Smoke the goose breast in a smoker filled with the merlot chips and lavender wood for 45 minutes.

In sauté pan, sear the goose breast, fat side down, for 8 minutes, until caramelized. Turn and sauté the other side of the breast for 4 minutes. Let rest for 15 minutes before slicing.

Using the goose legs and goose fat, prepare the goose confit. When the confit is done, remove the bone and shred the leg meat. Set the meat aside to be used to top the pain perdu and sliced goose breast.

To make the brioche, in a mixer, combine the flour, yeast, salt, butter, and sugar. Add the eggs and water and mix well with a dough hook on high speed until the dough becomes glossy and pulls completely away from the sides of the bowl. Refrigerate the dough for 4 hours. When ready to bake, preheat the oven to 350°. Roll the dough into a loaf, place in a bowl, cover, and allow to proof until the dough has tripled in size. Bake for 1 hour.

Toast 4 slices of the brioche bread. Place the toasted slices in a food processor and make bread crumbs.

To make the pain perdu, grill the corn over medium heat for about 15 minutes, turning while grilling. Remove the kernels and set aside. Measure out 2 tablespoons of the corn kernels and 2 tablespoons of the diced figs; reserve for the reduction. In a bowl, mix together the eggs, cream, and milk. Add the breadcrumbs, diced figs, and corn kernels. Season with salt and pepper. Heat the butter in a small nonstick pan over medium heat. Ladle 1-ounce portions of the mixture into the pan and cook for 1 minute on each side, until slightly brown.

To prepare the reduction, heat the goose fat in a medium pan and sauté all the vegetables in for 3 minutes. Add the apple. Sauté for 4 minutes, until it begins lightly sticking to the pan. Deglaze with wine. Reduce by one half, for about 2 minutes. Add the duck stock and reduce to 1 cup, about 10 minutes. Strain. Season with salt and pepper. Add the foie gras. Remove from the heat and mix well. Add the reserved 2 tablespoons of corn kernels and 2 tablespoons of diced figs to the sauce.

To serve, place the pain perdu in the center of the plate. Fan the goose breast slices on top and surrounding the pain perdu. Spoon the sauce over the duck breast and garnish with fresh lavender flowers.

Wine notes: Going with a kind of a chip off the old block,
I love Matanzas Creek Merlot with this goose breast.
Quelle surprise!

Asian-Style Barbecue Duck Rillette
on Crispy Brick Leaves with Daikon Relish

*H*ere's a dish that heads west to Europe—and keeps on going. It starts with a classic duck confit (I'm glad more and more chefs are rediscovering confit these days) and surrounds this with profound Asian flavors. Don't worry; you won't need to start with eel to make eel sauce—it's a product sold in most of the better Asian supermarkets.

SERVES 4

BRICK LEAVES

¾ CUP RENDERED DUCK FAT (PAGE 6)

Duck Rillette

1½ CUPS DUCK CONFIT (PAGE 6)

¼ CUP RENDERED DUCK FAT (PAGE 6)

1 TABLESPOON HOISIN SAUCE

1 TABLESPOON EEL SAUCE

½ TABLESPOON GARLIC JUICE
(JUICER EXTRACTED)

1 TABLESPOON GINGER JUICE
(JUICER EXTRACTED)

2 TABLESPOONS FINELY DICED SHALLOTS

1 TABLESPOON CILANTRO JUICE
(JUICER EXTRACTED)

1 TABLESPOON JALAPEÑO JUICE
(JUICER EXTRACTED)

1 TABLESPOON MINT JUICE
(JUICER EXTRACTED)

Daikon Relish

1 TEASPOON RICE WINE VINEGAR

1 TEASPOON FINELY GRATED LEMONGRASS

2 TABLESPOONS ASIAN FISH SAUCE

1 GARLIC CLOVE, CRUSHED AND FINELY
CHOPPED

1 TEASPOON PALM SUGAR

1 FRESH RED CHILE PEPPER, SEEDED AND

FINELY CHOPPED

2 TABLESPOONS SESAME OIL

1 DAIKON ROOT, PEELED AND FINELY
JULIENNED

1 CARROT, PEELED AND FINELY
JULIENNED

CILANTRO SPRIGS, FOR GARNISH
(OPTIONAL)

To prepare the brick leaves, preheat the oven to 300°. Cut 3 sheets of the brick leaves into 12 triangles each, for a total of 36. Stack sets of 3 triangles, brushing with duck fat and layering on top of each other. Bake the 12 stacks on a sheet pan for 5 to 7 minutes, until crispy. When removing from the sheet pan be careful not to break the delicate triangles.

To prepare the rillette, in a saucepan, heat the duck confit and duck fat. Sauté until the confit is crispy, approximately 2 minutes. Continue to stir and add the hoisin sauce, eel sauce, garlic juice, and ginger juice. Continue to cook for 2 minutes. Stir in the shallot, cilantro, jalapeño, and mint juices.

Layer the brick leaf triangles with the duck rillette, like napoleons. Each serving will have 3 triangles with 2 layers of rillette in between.

To prepare the relish, in a saucepan, combine all the ingredients except the sesame oil, daikon, and carrots and bring to a quick boil, about 3 minutes. Cool and add the oil.

Place the daikon and carrots in a mixing bowl. Pour the sauce over and allow the vegetables to marinate for 5 minutes.

To serve, place the rillette on the middle of the plate and pile relish next to it. Garnish with a cilantro sprig.

Wine notes: I think this dish wants a wine with acidity and spice,
so I'd go with an Alsatian Riesling.

Amish Chicken "Farci"
with Boursin Cheese, Leek Confit, and Young Vegetable Ragout and Pinot Noir Sauce

In my search for the best of everything, I've stumbled across these flavorful chickens raised by the Amish in Pennsylvania. The birds are entirely corn-fed, which gives them a very distinct taste—you might call it "essence of chicken." Still, the stuffing I've created pulls its weight in the dish, too, blending the wonderful seasoned cheese called boursin with leeks and bacon.

SERVES 4

Chicken

1 CUP FINELY JULIENNED
APPLE-SMOKED BACON

1 TABLESPOON BUTTER

1 CUP CHOPPED LEEKS,
WHITE PART ONLY

SEA SALT

CRACKED PEPPER

1 CUP BOURSIN CHEESE

4 AMISH CHICKEN BREASTS,
WITH BONE, SKIN ON

Young Vegetable Ragout

6 CUPS CHICKEN STOCK (PAGE 17),
REDUCED TO 2 CUPS

1 BABY CARROT

1 BABY YELLOW BEET

1 BABY RED BEET

1 BABY TURNIP

1 BABY CORN

1 BABY ZUCCHINI

1 BABY YELLOW SUNBURST

1 GREEN PATTYPAN SQUASH

1 CUP HARICOTS VERTS

1 CUP MOUSSERON MUSHROOMS

1 TABLESPOON TRUFFLE BUTTER

Pinot Noir Sauce

2 CUPS PINOT NOIR WINE

½ CUP DICED SHALLOTS

¼ CUP DICED CELERY

¼ CUP DICED CARROTS

1 TABLESPOON TRUFFLE BUTTER

FLOWERING THYME,
FOR GARNISH

To make the chicken, in a sauté pan, cook the bacon in the butter over medium heat, approximately 5 minutes. Transfer the bacon from the pan and set aside to cool. Pour the bacon fat into a small saucepot. Add the leeks, salt, and pepper. Cover and cook over low heat for 15 minutes, then set aside to cool. Chop the bacon into bits. Add the bacon bits and cheese to the leeks. Mix well and fill a pastry bag with the mixture.

Using a small knife, make a pocket in each chicken breast, slicing by the corner of the bone. Fill the pocket with the cheese mixture. Preheat the oven to 300°. In a large sauté pan, brown the chicken, skin-side first, about 3 minutes on each side. Finish the chicken by baking for 10 to 12 minutes. Set aside the sauté pan, which will be used to make the sauce.

To make the ragout, in a large saucepan, heat the chicken stock and simmer the carrot, yellow and red beets, turnip, and corn for 2 minutes. Add the zucchini, sunburst, pattypan, haricots verts, mushrooms, and truffle butter. Cook for 2 more minutes. Remove the vegetables with a slotted spoon and set aside. Reserve the chicken stock for use in the sauce.

(continued)

To make the sauce, deglaze the hot sauté pan used for the chicken with the wine. Add the shallots, celery, and carrots. Reduce over high heat by one third, approximately 2 minutes. Add the chicken stock from the vegetable ragout and reduce by one third, approximately 5 minutes. Strain. Whisk in the truffle butter.

Add the baked chicken breasts and drippings to the pan of sauce so that the chicken will absorb the sauce until ready to serve.

To assemble each individual serving, place the ragout of vegetables on the center of the plate. Lay a chicken breast on top of the vegetables. Garnish with a thyme sprig.

Wine notes: To pick up notes from the sauce,
I like to serve El Molino Pinot Noir.

Duck Confit & Goat Cheese
in Phyllo Galette with Smoky Morel Jus

*H*ere's a dish that has it all, and it's one of my heartiest. Needless to say, it sells better in the wintertime than during the long, hot summer of New Orleans. Occasionally it does get cold and wet here too, making room for dishes like this. The goat cheese is wonderful with the duck confit. And I can't say enough about the smoky morel jus, which uses mushrooms taken from ground that has been burned to give them that smoky flavor.

Talk about going to any lengths for a wonderful taste!

SERVES 4

Galette

2 CUPS DUCK CONFIT
(PAGE 6)

1 CUP GOAT CHEESE

1 TABLESPOON CHOPPED FRESH THYME

1 POUND PHYLLO DOUGH SHEETS

¼ CUP BUTTER, MELTED

Morel Jus

4 TABLESPOONS VEGETABLE OIL

4 TABLESPOONS DICED SHALLOTS

2 TABLESPOONS DICED CARROTS

2 TABLESPOONS DICED CELERY

½ CUP RED WINE

4 CUPS VEAL STOCK (PAGE 18)

1 CUP SMOKY MOREL MUSHROOMS,
CLEANED AND HALVED

1 TABLESPOON TRUFFLE BUTTER

YELLOW AND RED TEARDROP TOMATOES,
FOR GARNISH

MICRO CELERY, FOR GARNISH

(continued)

(Duck Confit and Goat Cheese continued)

To make the galette, prepare the duck confit, removing the bones and fat from the duck legs and shredding the meat finely with a small fork. In a small mixing bowl, fold in the goat cheese and thyme.

Preheat the oven to 350°. Brush 1 sheet of the phyllo with melted butter. Repeat the process 3 times until you have stacked 4 layers of phyllo. To assemble (see illustrations on page 121), cut the layered phyllo sheets in half and then into 2-inch strips. Line a ring mold with the phyllo strips, using 4 strips per ring in a crisscross fashion, as illustrated on page 121. Spoon the shredded duck/goat cheese mixture into the mold and fold the strips over the top. Remove the ring mold and repeat the process to make 3 more galettes. Set on a sheet pan and bake for 8 minutes, until golden brown.

To make the morel jus, in a sauté pan, heat 2 tablespoons of the oil and sauté 2 tablespoons of the shallots and the carrots and celery for 2 minutes. Add the wine and stock and reduce to 1 cup, approximately 15 minutes.

In a second sauté pan, heat the remaining 2 tablespoons oil and sauté the remaining shallots and the mushrooms for 5 minutes. Add the veal stock and finish with the truffle butter.

To serve, spread a large spoonful of the morel jus on each plate and place a galette in the center. Garnish with micro celery and teardrop tomatoes.

Wine notes: I would suggest a big California cabernet for this big, hearty main course—maybe an Araujo or Silver Oak Alexander Valley.

1.

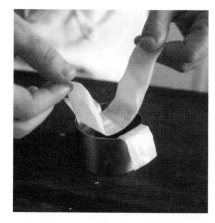

2.

3.

4.

MEAT & GAME

Cumin-Rubbed Pork Tenderloin
with Hearts of Palm–Tamarind Relish, and Pork and Casaba Croquette

This dish tastes very New World to me, and, of course, very Hispanic. It's one of the few dishes that pays tribute to all the chefs I know who are doing such wonderful work in the Nuevo Latino mode. The use of pork reflects its status as the favored meat of places such as Cuba and Puerto Rico, and even of Caribbean islands—such as Jamaica—where the Spanish influence is less evident. Cumin (*comino* in Spanish) is a signature flavor of many Hispanic dishes. I trust you'll find this pork tenderloin a lot more subtle—and satisfying.

SERVES 8

Pork and Casaba Croquette

<u>MARINADE</u>

1 ONION, PEELED AND CHOPPED

6 CLOVES GARLIC

½ CUP CHOPPED FRESH CILANTRO

2 TABLESPOONS SALT

1 TABLESPOON FRESHLY
GROUND PEPPER

1 BAY LEAF

½ CUP FRESHLY SQUEEZED
LIME JUICE

½ CUP FRESHLY SQUEEZED LEMON JUICE

¼ CUP DARK RUM

3 QUARTS PORK STOCK
(FOLLOW DUCK STOCK RECIPE ON PAGE
17, USING PORK INSTEAD OF DUCK)
OR WATER

1 TABLESPOON CHOPPED
FRESH THYME

1 TABLESPOON CHOPPED
FRESH MINT

1 (2-POUND) PORK BUTT,
WITH FAT TRIMMED

CROQUETTE

1 POUND CASAVA MELON

2 TABLESPOONS SCOTCH BONNET PEPPER
OIL (AVAILABLE IN GOURMET SHOPS)

3 SHALLOTS, FINELY CHOPPED

2 CLOVES GARLIC, CRUSHED

SALT

PEPPER

¼ CUP CHOPPED FRESH CILANTRO

1 TABLESPOON CHOPPED FRESH MINT

3 GREEN ONIONS, FINELY CHOPPED,
GREEN AND WHITE PARTS

1 CUP ALL-PURPOSE FLOUR

2 EGGS, BEATEN

2 CUPS BREADCRUMBS

3 CUPS VEGETABLE OIL

Hearts of Palm–Tamarind Relish

1 TABLESPOON TAMARIND PURÉE

2 TABLESPOONS FRESHLY SQUEEZED
LEMON JUICE

1 TEASPOON GINGER JUICE, JUICER
EXTRACTED

½ CUP PEANUT OIL

1 JALAPEÑO PEPPER, SEEDED AND JUICED

4 CUPS PORK STOCK
(FOLLOW DUCK STOCK RECIPE ON
PAGE 17, USING PORK INSTEAD OF DUCK)

2 POUNDS FRESH HEARTS OF PALM

1 TEASPOON CHOPPED FRESH MINT

1 TEASPOON CHOPPED FRESH CILANTRO

Pork Tenderloin

8 (4-OUNCE) PIECES PORK TENDERLOIN

¼ CUP VEGETABLE OIL

2 TABLESPOONS CUMIN POWDER

1 TABLESPOON CHOPPED FRESH THYME

To make the marinade, blend all the ingredients together in a blender. Marinate the pork butt for 24 hours in refrigerator.

Preheat the oven to 275°. Place the pork in a roasting pan and cover with the marinade. Cover the pan with aluminum foil. Braise in the oven for 2 hours, then turn the pork butt over and braise for another 2 hours. The meat should be falling off the bone. Remove from the oven and allow to cool. Shred the pork meat with a fork and set aside.

(continued)

To prepare the croquette, boil the casava in 2 quarts of water for about 20 minutes, until soft. Drain and peel. Purée the casava and set aside.

In a large pan, heat the pepper oil over medium heat and sauté the shallots and garlic for about 3 minutes. Add the shredded pork and sauté for 3 more minutes. Add the casava purée and season with salt and pepper to taste. Remove from the heat and allow to cool. When cool, mix in the cilantro, mint, and green onion.

Place the mixture in a pastry bag. Cut a 1-inch hole in the tip of the bag. Squeeze the mixture out onto a sheet pan in 24 3-inch-long cylinder-shaped croquettes. Place the flour in a bowl and lightly coat the croquettes with the flour. Dip the croquettes in the egg and coat with the breadcrumbs. Heat the vegetable oil in a deep fryer or pan; it should be 6 inches deep. Fry the croquettes 3 to 4 minutes until golden brown.

To make the relish, in a mixing bowl, mix together the tamarind purée, lemon juice, ginger juice, and oil. Add the jalapeño juice a little at a time, tasting after each addition, until the desired amount of heat is achieved. Add the hearts of palm, mint, and cilantro and mix thoroughly. Bring the pork stock to a simmer over medium heat. Add the hearts of palm and simmer for 20 minutes. Remove form heat and allow to cool. Take out the hearts of palm and julienne them.

To prepare the tenderloin, rub with the oil. Sprinkle the cumin and thyme on top. Grill the pork on a grill preheated to medium for 8 minutes, until cooked medium. It should be moist; do not overcook.

To assemble each individual serving, place a piece of pork tenderloin in the center of the plate. Add 3 croquettes. Place relish on top.

Wine notes: This pairing is a challenge, since you can enjoy this dish with either white or red. I'd pull out a bottle of Robert Mondavi's Landmark Fumé Blanc, and simply enjoy. In order to complement the dish as a whole—the spice on the pork, the sweetness of the casava, and the nuttiness of the relish—a full-bodied American chardonnay like Kistler will do the trick.

A Study of Lamb…
Roasted Rack of Lamb with a Lamb Confit–Caramelized Spaghetti Squash Galette, Merguez Sausage, and Bone-Marrow Flan

*T*his signature dish (or collection of dishes) is not so much difficult as extended. It's kind of a master's thesis on lamb cookery, stemming as it does from my wish to use as many parts of the lamb on one plate as possible. When it comes to lamb, I hate to waste anything. As it turns out, I don't waste much: showcasing the rack, of course, but also producing a savory confit, a delicate galette, and some well-spiced Moroccan merguez sausage. Even the lamb marrow gets used, bringing a unique taste to the flan.

An alternative to making the merguez sausage from scratch is to purchase it ready-made at a specialty store. One brand I like is Marcel & Henri.

SERVES 8

Bone-Marrow Flan

½ CUP HEAVY CREAM

½ CUP MILK

2 CUPS LAMB STOCK (PAGE 18)

4 OUNCES LAMB MARROW, REMOVED FROM ABOUT 10 3-INCH LAMB BONE PIECES (HAVE YOUR BUTCHER DO IT FOR YOU)

SEA SALT

PEPPER

2 EGGS

2 TEASPOONS UNSALTED BUTTER, FOR FLAN MOLDS

(continued)

Lamb Confit–Caramelized Spaghetti Squash Galette

¼ CUP OLIVE OIL

¼ CUP CHOPPED FRESH GARLIC

½ CUP CHOPPED FRESH THYME

3 TEASPOONS CRUSHED BLACK PEPPER

3 TEASPOONS SEA SALT

2 POUNDS LAMB FROM LEG MEAT

3 QUARTS LAMB FAT

2 SPAGHETTI SQUASHES, CUT IN HALF

1 CUP ALL-PURPOSE FLOUR

1 CUP PANKO

3 EGGS, BEATEN

Rack of Lamb

1 RACK OF LAMB

SEA SALT

PEPPER

2 TABLESPOONS DIJON MUSTARD

¼ CUP CHOPPED FRESH THYME

Merguez Sausage

HARISSA

6 TABLESPOONS OLIVE OIL

2 TABLESPOONS CRUSHED FRESH GARLIC

½ CUP DICED LEEKS

½ CUP DICED CELERY

½ CUP DICED SHALLOTS

½ CUP DICED CARROT

2 CAYENNE PEPPERS, SEEDED

½ TEASPOON CORIANDER SEEDS

½ TEASPOON FINELY CHOPPED FRESH MINT

½ TEASPOON CARAWAY SEEDS

½ TEASPOON SEA SALT

½ TEASPOON BLACK PEPPER

SAUSAGE

1 POUND GROUND LAMB, AT LEAST 15% FAT

1 TABLESPOON FRESH THYME

1 TABLESPOON FRESH, CHOPPED ROSEMARY

4 FEET OF LAMB CASING (ASK YOUR BUTCHER)

To make the flan, preheat the oven to 300°. In a large sauce pot, heat the cream and milk over medium heat until just boiling. Transfer from the heat. In a separate sauce pot, heat the stock over medium heat until it reaches a slow boil. Add the marrow and cook for 5 minutes, until tender. With a slotted spoon, transfer the marrow to the milk mixture. Return to the burner and cook for 3 minutes on medium heat.

Place in a blender and purée. Season with salt and pepper. Add the eggs to the hot mixture and blend until smooth. Strain through a fine sieve. Grease 8 flan molds with butter and fill with the purée. Bake for 35 minutes in a bain-marie, or water bath.

To prepare the confit, combine the olive oil, garlic, ¼ cup of the thyme, 2 teaspoons of the pepper, and 2 teaspoons of the salt. Coat the lamb meat with the mixture and marinate, refrigerated, for 24 hours.

Preheat the oven to 225°. Place the lamb in a roasting pan and cover with the lamb fat. Cover with aluminum foil and bake for 10 hours. Remove the lamb with a slotted spoon and shred. Reserve the fat for the galette.

To prepare the galette, preheat the oven to 300°. Bake the spaghetti squash for 15 minutes. Remove and allow to cool. Scoop out the inner pulp with a fork.

In a sauté pan over medium heat, cook the shredded lamb until lightly browned. When the meat begins sticking to the pan, add the squash pulp to clean the bottom of the pan and cook for 10 to 15 minutes, until slightly caramelized. Taste and season with salt and pepper if necessary.

Press the squash mixture into a 2½-inch-wide ring mold to shape a galette.

In a mixing bowl combine the flour, panko, and eggs. Coat the galette with the mixture. Place 1 cup of the lamb fat in a sauté pan and heat on a medium flame. Sauté the galette until golden brown on both sides, about 30 seconds on each side.

To prepare the rack of lamb, preheat the oven to 350°. Season the lamb with salt and pepper. In a pan over medium heat, sear the lamb on both sides until golden brown, approximately 5 minutes. Allow to cool. Brush the lamb with the mustard and crust with the thyme.

Roast the lamb for 15 minutes, until medium rare. Transfer from the oven and allow the lamb to rest for 3 minutes prior to cutting chop portions.

(continued)

To prepare the harissa for the sausage, in a large sauté pan, heat the olive oil over a high flame. Add the garlic, leeks, celery, shallots, carrots, and peppers. Cook for 5 to 7 minutes, until done. Transfer to a food processor and purée. Allow to cool. Mix in the coriander seeds, mint, caraway seeds, salt, and pepper. Refrigerate in a covered glass bowl for 1 hour. (Leftover keeps refrigerated for 2 to 3 weeks.)

Mix the lamb with the thyme, rosemary, and ½ cup of the harissa. Sauté a small piece of the lamb mixture in a pan to taste for seasoning. Add seasoning as necessary.

Prepare a lamb casing by washing it under running water to open it up. Fill a cookie press with the meat mixture. Press to add meat into the casing until about 5 inches of the casing are filled. Turn off the press and twist the sausage. Tie each end of the casing. Repeat until the long link is complete. Cut off each individual sausage with scissors.

For final cooking and presentation, preheat the oven to 350°. Finish the galettes by baking for 5 minutes.

Wine notes: How about pairing this dish with a Rhone from Cornas? You'll love these big reds with enough peppery aftertaste to almost become another spice for the lamb. One of my favorite choices is the Domaine Auguste Clape.

Pinwheel of Roasted Lamb Loin
with Saffron Couscous-Ratatouille

*T*hough couscous and ratatouille are both excellent on their own, smiling at each other across the Mediterranean, I mix them together here to form a very special cake. The cake is, in turn, cut in circles, becoming a building block for slices of the seared lamb loin—giving the visual impression of a child's pinwheel. The sauce starts as a cabernet vinaigrette, then takes on a new character when it's emulsified with lamb stock and rosemary. The finished sauce makes me dream of Provence!

SERVES 4

Lamb

1 POUND LAMB LOIN

SEA SALT

PEPPER

1 TABLESPOON CHOPPED FRESH THYME

Ratatouille

½ CUP DICED EGGPLANT, PURPLE PEEL ONLY

½ CUP OVEN-DRIED TOMATOES OIL (PAGE 2)

½ CUP DICED RED ONION

½ CUP DICED ZUCCHINI, GREEN PEEL ONLY

½ CUP DICED YELLOW SQUASH, YELLOW PEEL ONLY

1 TABLESPOON FINELY CHOPPED FRESH GARLIC

½ CUP DICED RED, YELLOW, AND GREEN BELL PEPPERS

½ CUP FINELY DICED OVEN-DRIED TOMATOES (PAGE 2)

(continued)

(Roasted Lamb Loin continued)

Saffron Couscous

1 CUP HEAVY CREAM

10 THREADS SAFFRON

12 OVEN-DRIED TOMATOES (PAGE 2)

5 CUPS DUCK STOCK (PAGE 17)

SEA SALT

PEPPER

3 EGG YOLKS, BEATEN

2 CUPS UNCOOKED COUSCOUS

Vinaigrette

2 CUPS CABERNET SAUVIGNON WINE

2 TABLESPOONS CHOPPED SHALLOTS

5 CUPS LAMB STOCK (PAGE 18)

2 SPRIGS ROSEMARY

1 CUP OLIVE OIL

¼ CUP EXTRA-VIRGIN OLIVE OIL

SEA SALT

PEPPER

To prepare the lamb, preheat the oven to 350°. Season the lamb loin with salt and pepper. In a sauté pan on high heat, sear the lamb on all sides, approximately 3 to 4 minutes. Allow to cool. Rub the loin with the thyme and bake for 10 minutes. Allow the meat to rest for 3 minutes before slicing into 20 equal slices.

To prepare the ratatouille, in a large sauté pan, sauté the eggplant in the tomato oil for 2 minutes. Add the onion and continue to sauté for 1 minute. Add the remaining vegetables and sauté for 3 minutes. Remove from the heat and allow to cool. Set the ratatouille aside to use in the couscous.

To prepare the couscous, in a saucepan, bring the cream to a boil. Add the saffron threads and boil for 1 minute. Add the tomatoes and stock. Season with salt and pepper. Boil for 5 minutes. Transfer the hot liquid to a large mixing bowl. Whisk in the egg yolks and then add the couscous. Add the ratatouille. Season with salt and pepper to taste.

Preheat the oven to 300°. Transfer the couscous-ratatouille to a 9 by 12 by 3-inch baking pan and bake for 25 minutes. Remove from the oven and let cool. Using a 5-inch round cutter, cut out 4 couscous cakes.

To make the vinaigrette, lower the oven heat to 275°. In a saucepan over medium heat, combine the wine and shallots and cook until reduced to 1 cup. Strain through a sieve and combine with the lamb stock in a saucepan. Continue cooking until reduced to 1 cup. Strain again.

Roast the rosemary in the oven until lightly dried, approximately 2 minutes. Add to the stock reduction and steep for 10 minutes. Strain and transfer the liquid to a blender. Emulsify the stock with the olive oils and season with salt and pepper.

To assemble each individual serving, place a couscous cake on the center of the plate. Arrange 5 slices of lamb on the couscous cake in a pinwheel shape. Drizzle with warm vinaigrette and serve immediately.

Wine notes: I'd like a red Sancerre, please. And make mine a Lucien Crochet Clos du Roy.

Noisette of Pancetta-Wrapped
Kobe Beef with Chanterelles

If you have ever enjoyed oh-so-classic Beef Wellington, you can imagine how I began dreaming up this dish. What really got me going, though, was the Kobe beef, with its tender texture and delicate flavor produced by the lifetime of pampering these cattle receive in Japan. I'm told they even listen to soft, classical music all the time! Well, after all that, you can't just toss this beef on the grill on Sunday afternoon. I replace traditional puff pastry with lightly salty Italian pancetta and pliable slices of potato. As for the sauce, honestly, I love chanterelles with just about anything.

SERVES 4

Beef

2 CUPS RENDERED DUCK FAT (PAGE 6)

2 IDAHO POTATOES, SKIN ON, CUT INTO ¼-INCH SLICES

24 OUNCES CENTER-CUT KOBE BEEF, QUARTERED

SEA SALT

PEPPER

½ POUND PANCETTA, FROZEN (FOR EASE OF SLICING)

Chanterelle Sauce

3 TABLESPOONS RENDERED DUCK FAT (PAGE 6)

1 POUND CHANTERELLE MUSHROOMS

3 TABLESPOONS CHOPPED SHALLOTS

½ CUP CABERNET SAUVIGNON WINE

4 SPRIGS THYME, FOR GARNISH

In a sauté pan over high heat, sauté the potatoes in the duck fat for 1 minute, until soft, not crispy. The potatoes must be lightly cooked, so that they do not change color, and stay soft enough to be pliant. With a slotted spoon, remove from the fat and place on paper towels to drain and dry.

Season the beef with salt and pepper. In a sauté pan over high heat, sear the beef on all sides.

To form the noisette, thinly slice the pancetta. Wrap the beef first with the pancetta, then with potato slices. Wrap the entire noisette very tightly with plastic wrap, forming a sausage shape. Refrigerate for 3 hours to set the shape.

Preheat the oven to 350° and unwrap the noisette. In a sauté pan, heat ½ cup of the duck fat over medium heat. Using tongs, carefully place the noisette in the fat and cook lightly, just enough to give the potato wrapping a bit of color. Transfer to a sheet pan and bake for 10 minutes until golden brown. Transfer to a cutting board and slice the noisette into 20 slices.

To make the sauce, in a sauté pan, heat the duck fat and sauté the chanterelles and shallots for 5 minutes. Drain off the duck fat and add the wine. Reduce to one third.

To assemble each individual serving, arrange 5 noisettes of beef on the plate in a pinwheel. Drizzle chanterelle sauce around the plate and garnish with a sprig of thyme.

Wine notes: Try a Leonetti cabernet from Walla Walla, Washington. How often in life can you order Walla Walla wine?

Roasted Farm-Raised Venison
on a Cranberry-Thyme Mashed Potato and White Corn Reduction

I invested considerable time in creating the ultimate mashed potatoes for this terrific venison—potatoes that would respect the pure flavors of the game. Are you ready for cranberry-thyme mashed potatoes? And you'd better not miss out on what happens when the potatoes mingle with a white corn reduction made real by an intense demiglace of venison.

SERVES 6

24 OUNCES VENISON FILET

Cranberry-Thyme Mashed Potato

2 SHALLOTS, CHOPPED

2 TABLESPOONS VEGETABLE OIL

½ CUP FRESH CRANBERRIES

1 TABLESPOON SUGAR

1 CUP BLOND CHICKEN STOCK (PAGE 17)

1 TABLESPOON CHOPPED FRESH THYME

3 CUPS GARLIC MASHED POTATOES
(PAGE 146) WITHOUT THE GARLIC

White Corn Reduction

2 EARS OF CORN

4 SHALLOTS, FINELY CHOPPED

2 TABLESPOONS GRAPESEED OIL

½ CUP FINELY CHOPPED
APPLE-SMOKED BACON

1 CUP CABERNET WINE

4 CUPS VENISON STOCK
(PAGE 19, REDUCED BY ½)

Sear the venison filet in a sauté pan over medium heat for 5 minutes on each side. Finish in a 350° oven for 7 minutes. The filet will be medium-rare. Allow the meat to rest for 4 minutes before slicing. Slice into 6 portions.

To prepare the mashed potatoes, sauté the shallots in oil over medium heat for about 2 minutes. Add the cranberries and sauté for another 2 minutes. Add the sugar and cook for 5 minutes. Add the chicken stock and bring to a boil. Remove from heat. Allow to cool. Purée. Add the chopped thyme. Fold the mixture into the mashed potatoes.

To prepare the corn reduction, grill the corn on a preheated grill for 15 minutes over medium heat. Remove the husks and reserve.

Sauté the shallots in oil over medium heat for 2 minutes. Add the corn and sauté for 2 more minutes. Add the bacon and cook for 5 minutes. Deglaze the pan with wine. Add the reduced venison stock, or demiglace, and bring to a boil. Decrease to a simmer and remove all excess fat. Blend and strain. Season to taste.

To serve, place a scoop of mashed potato in the middle of each plate. Place sliced venison around the potatoes and drizzle corn reduction over everything.

Wine notes: A 1997 L'École No. 41 "Apogee" Meritage
would complement this dish.

Double Chop of Wild Boar
with Three Potato–Goat Cheese Terrine

The double chop provides a more substantial serving than a single, so I prefer to serve wild boar this way. Cippolini are small Italian onions, just a little bit sweet until they get balanced by the balsamic vinegar and garlic.

SERVES 8

Cipollini Onion Confit

2 POUNDS PEELED CIPOLLINI ONIONS

4 CUPS POMACE OLIVE OIL

¼ CUP CHOPPED FRESH THYME

2 TABLESPOONS CHOPPED FRESH GARLIC

½ CUP BALSAMIC VINEGAR

1 TABLESPOON SALT

½ TEASPOON FRESHLY CRACKED PEPPER

Wild Boar

¼ CUP BACON FAT

2 WILD BOAR CHOPS

1 CUP CIPOLLINI ONION CONFIT PURÉE (FROM ONION CONFIT, ABOVE)

½ CUP DIJON MUSTARD

2 POUNDS CAUL FAT

Goat Cheese Terrine

1 POUND YUKON GOLD POTATOES

1 POUND LAROTTE POTATOES

1 POUND BEINJEE POTATOES

5 CUPS PORK FAT FROM RENDERED PORK

1 POUND WILD BOAR BACON, SLICED

4 TABLESPOONS CHOPPED FRESH THYME

SALT

PEPPER

1 CUP GOAT CHEESE

Wild Boar Jus

3 CUPS RED WINE

2 SHALLOTS, DICED

1 QUART BOAR STOCK (FOLLOW LAMB STOCK RECIPE ON PAGE 18, SUBSTITUTING BOAR FOR LAMB)

1 POUND WATERCRESS

To make the onion confit, preheat the oven to 250°. Place all the ingredients in a medium-sized pot over medium heat and simmer. Cover with foil and place in the oven for 2 hours. Remove, strain, and reserve the liquid to dress the watercress. Purée the onion in a food processer to a smooth paste. Let cool and refrigerate. Reserve for use with the boar chops.

To prepare the wild boar, preheat the oven to 350°. Heat half of the bacon fat in a sauté pan over medium heat. Sear all around the boar chops for about 5 minutes, until golden brown. Remove from the pan and let cool for 5 minutes before cutting each chop into 4 pieces. Remove the bones and discard. Brush with the mustard and spread one tablespoon of the onion purée on each chop. Wrap caul fat tightly around each chop to make a round shape. This may be done up to one day in advance.

To prepare the terrine, preheat the oven to 300°. Without removing the skin, cut the potatoes into ⅛-inch-thick slices. Heat the pork fat in a medium-sized pan over medium heat. Blanch the potatoes in small batches in the pork fat, about 3 minutes for each batch or until soft. Remove from the fat and allow to cool.

Line a terrine mold with the boar bacon, overlapping the slices. Layer ⅕ of the potato slices on top. Sprinkle with thyme, salt, and pepper. Layer goat cheese on top. Repeat until the ingredients are used up. Cover the terrine with foil and place in a bain marie. Bake in the oven for 30 minutes. Remove from the oven and let cool. Refrigerate for at least 2 hours. Slice into 1½-inch portions. Bake again in the oven for 5 minutes just before serving.

To prepare the jus, heat the wine and the shallots over medium heat for about 15 minutes, until reduced to about 1 cup. Strain and add the liquid to the boar stock. Reduce over medium heat for 25 minutes until about one-third the original, or until it coats the back of a spoon.

To serve, increase the oven temperature to 350°. Heat the remaining bacon fat from the wild boar over medium heat in a large sauté pan and sear the wrapped chops in bacon fat for 3 to 4 minutes, until golden brown. Remove from the pan and finish in the oven for 7 minutes. Wild boar needs to be served medium to medium-rare. Place warmed terrine slice on the plate next to a boar chop. Drizzle boar jus over the chop. In a separate bowl, toss watercress with ¼ cup of the liquid reserved from the onion confit.

Wine notes: Iris Rideau's 1998 Syrah has a spicy perfumed nose with just the right hints of currants, blackberry, and anise.

Pig Trotter on Mâche
with Crispy Bacon and Port Wine Vinaigrette

*B*ecause pig's feet have relatively little meat, I always use the entire shank. In this dish, in fact, I combine the shank meat with the braised sweetbreads and some fresh sage for fragrance. The port wine reduction kicks in the perfect balance of sweet and pungent flavors, while the mâche stands in for the traditional beans or lentils.

SERVES 4

Pig Trotter

1 POUND PIG TROTTERS WITH SHANK

4 CARROTS

1 CELERY

2 ONIONS

1 LEEK, WHITE AND GREEN PARTS

2 TABLESPOONS VEGETABLE OIL

1 CUP FRESH PARSLEY

1 CUP FRESH THYME

2 CLOVES GARLIC

8 CUPS VEAL STOCK (PAGE 18)

Sweetbread Stuffing

5 SLICES APPLE-SMOKED BACON

2 CARROTS

1 STALK OF CELERY

2 SHALLOTS

4 POACHED AND PRESSED SWEETBREADS (PAGE 151)

SALT

PEPPER

1 POUND CAUL FAT (SOAKED AND DRAINED)

6 SAGE LEAVES

Port Wine Reduction

3 CUPS PORT WINE

1 CUP TROTTER LIQUID

½ CUP GRAPESEED OIL

SALT

PEPPER

MÂCHE, FOR GARNISH

To prepare the pig trotters, preheat the oven to 275°. Slice the trotters lengthwise without cutting all the way through. Peel and chop all the vegetables into a mirepoix. Heat the oil in a braising pan over medium heat, and braise the mirepoix for 10 minutes. Remove from the heat, and add the parsley, thyme, and garlic. Place the trotters in the pan and spoon the vegetables over the top. Pour in the veal stock and simmer for 10 minutes. Cover and place in the oven for up to 6 hours or until the meat falls easily off the bone. Remove from the oven and allow to cool. Remove the skin in one piece if possible, scrape it clean, and place on parchment paper on a sheet pan. Refrigerate to use later for wrapping. Remove the meat from the bone and shred. Put it in the refrigerator also. Reserve the liquid for the wine reduction. Discard the bones and vegetables.

To prepare the sweetbread stuffing, increase the oven temperature to 350°. Cut the bacon into thin strips and bake for 5 minutes, until crispy. Remove and reserve for garnish. Put 2 tablespoons of the bacon fat aside to be used later. Heat the rest of the fat in a pan over medium heat. Peel and dice the vegetables. Dice the sweetbread. Sauté the vegetables and the sweetbread in the fat for about 5 minutes, until lightly caramelized. Allow to cool.

Reduce the oven temperature to 300°. In a large mixing bowl, mix the sweetbreads with the shredded trotter meat. Season with salt and pepper. Remove the trotter skin from the refrigerator and allow to soften at room temperature. Place 2 layers of caul fat flat on a cutting board. Layer sage leaves on top. Layer trotter skin on top. Place the sweetbread and shredded trotter meat mixture in the middle and wrap tightly like a sausage. Heat the 2 tablespoons of the reserved bacon fat in a large pan over low heat. Sauté the trotter sausage for about 5 minutes, turning on all sides until lightly brown. Remove any excess fat from the pan and place in the oven for 15 minutes.

To make the port wine reduction, heat the wine in a medium-sized pan on medium heat for 10 minutes until reduced by one-third. Add the trotter liquid and reduce by one-half. Remove from the heat. Add the grapeseed oil and emulsify using a hand blender while still hot. Season to taste.

To serve, place the trotter next to the mâche. Drizzle on port wine vinaigrette, then place the crispy bacon strips on top.

Wine notes: For this, I would recommend a cabernet sauvignon from the Eisele Vineyard, of Araujo Winery. It has layers of flavors that coat the palate.

Venison Osso-Buco
on Celery Root and Granny Smith Apple Purée with Oven-Dried Shallot Jus

I know Italians nearly always make osso-buco with veal shank, and I really love it when they make it for me. But that didn't stop me from wondering if venison would be every bit as good—maybe better. On top of the joys of venison itself, I think you'll appreciate how the celery root contributes an earthiness to this dish, balancing the tartness of the Granny Smith apple and the caramelized sweetness of the oven-dried shallot jus.

SERVES 4

Oven-Dried Shallots

2 CUPS OLIVE OIL

20 SHALLOTS, PEELED

10 SPRIGS THYME

½ CUP CHOPPED GARLIC

1 TEASPOON SALT

1 TEASPOON PEPPER

1 TABLESPOON SUGAR

Venison Osso-Buco

6 CUPS RED BURGUNDY WINE

2 CUPS CHOPPED CELERY

6 CARROTS, PEELED AND CHOPPED

4 ONIONS, PEELED AND CHOPPED

2 BAY LEAVES

1 TEASPOON CRACKED AND CRUSHED JUNIPER BERRIES

6 SPRIGS THYME

2 SPRIGS ROSEMARY

2 CLOVES GARLIC

12 (3-OUNCE) VENISON SHANKS

8 CUPS VENISON STOCK (PAGE 19)

SALT

PEPPER

½ CUP FLOUR

1 SPRIG TARRAGON

Celery Root and Apple Purée

2 CELERY ROOTS

2 GRANNY SMITH APPLES

¼ CUP OIL FROM OVEN-DRIED
SHALLOTS, ABOVE

¼ CUP HEAVY CREAM

SALT

PEPPER

8 BABY SQUASHES

8 ASPARAGUS SPEARS

1 TABLESPOON OLIVE OIL

To prepare the shallots, preheat the oven to 200°. Pour the olive oil into a sheet pan. Add the shallots, thyme, and garlic. Sprinkle with the salt, pepper, and sugar. Bake for 1 hour. Turn the shallots over and bake for another hour. Note: This recipe makes 20 shallots, but only 5 will be used for the jus. Leftover shallots are wonderful on salads or in a vinaigrette.

To prepare the osso-buco, make a marinade in a bowl by combining the wine, 1 cup of the celery, half of the carrots, half of the onion, the bay leaves, juniper berries, 2 sprigs of thyme, 1 sprig of rosemary, and the garlic. Add the venison and refrigerate for 24 hours.

Transfer the venison to a cutting board. Transfer the marinade to a pot. Cook over medium heat until reduced by half. Add marinade to venison stock and set aside.

Preheat the oven to 300°. Season the venison with salt and pepper and lightly dust with flour. In a large saucepan over medium heat, sear the venison until it is golden brown. Place the venison in a roasting pan and pour the venison stock and reduced marinade over it. Place around the meat the remaining 1 cup of celery, carrots, onions, thyme, and rosemary, and the tarragon. Cover with aluminum foil. Braise in the oven for approximately 3 hours. The meat should be tender and easily removed from the bone.

(continued)

Remove the venison from the stock. Strain the stock through a fine sieve and reduce to 4 cups. Add 5 oven-dried shallots. Purée in a blender. Season with salt and pepper. Pour over the venison.

To prepare the pureé, preheat the oven to 300°. Put the celery roots and apples in a pan and lightly brush with oil. Roast for 30 minutes, removing apples after 10 minutes. Using a towel, peel the hot celery roots and apples and purée in a blender with the cream. Season with salt and pepper.

Blanch the squash and asparagus in boiling water for 2 minutes. In a sauté pan over medium heat, heat the olive oil and butter. Sauté the squash and asparagus for 1 minute. Season with salt and pepper.

To assemble each individual serving, place the celery root and apple purée in a bowl. Place 3 pieces of osso-buco on top. Pour sauce over the meat. Garnish with baby squash and asparagus.

Wine notes: Let's go Italian. I'd pour a Barolo or one
of those big red wines from Tuscany.

Burgundy Braised Rabbit
with Garlic Mashed Potatoes

In this dish, the word Burgundy honors both the wine and the region.
It even pays homage to a traditional recipe—most Americans have heard of Beef
Bourguignonne. In this variant, I marinate farm-raised rabbit in burgundy
(the wine, not the region, unfortunately) for 24 hours along with onions, carrots,
and celery. I'd say it's like a Drunken Rabbit, except better. Hint: It's almost impos-
sible to braise this rabbit too slowly, as the cooking time is what lets the deep flavors
develop. Of course, that's not telling a Burgundian anything he didn't know!

SERVES 8

Marinade

1½ (750 ML) BOTTLES LIGHT BURGUNDY
WINE OR CALIFORNIA PINOT NOIR

3 CARROTS, PEELED AND CHOPPED

1 STALK CELERY, CHOPPED

2 YELLOW ONIONS, CHOPPED

2 BAY LEAVES

1 CLOVE GARLIC, CRUSHED

½ POUND BACON, CHOPPED

Braised Rabbit

3 WHOLE RABBITS

SALT

PEPPER

FLOUR

3 CARROTS, PEELED AND
CHOPPED

½ CELERY STALK

2 ONIONS, CHOPPED

1 BAY LEAF

2 SPRIGS THYME

1 POUND BACON

2 QUARTS RABBIT STOCK (PAGE 18)

(continued)

Garlic Mashed Potatoes

10 YUKON GOLD POTATOES

2 CLOVES GARLIC, FINELY CRUSHED

1 SHALLOT, FINELY CHOPPED

3 TABLESPOONS BUTTER

5 TABLESPOONS HEAVY CREAM

SALT

PEPPER

2 POUNDS PEARL ONIONS

24 BABY CARROTS

To make the marinade, combine all the ingredients in a large bowl. Cut each rabbit into 8 pieces. Marinate the rabbit in the refrigerator for 24 hours. Remove the rabbit from the marinade. In a saucepan, heat the marinade over low heat until reduced to one quarter. Strain through a fine sieve and reserve.

Season the rabbit with salt and pepper. Dust with a small amount of flour. In a large skillet over medium heat, sear the rabbit until golden brown, approximately 5 minutes. Be careful not to burn it; that would make the sauce bitter.

Preheat the oven to 300°. Place the rabbit in a large baking dish and cover with the marinade. Add the carrots, celery, onions, bay leaf, thyme, bacon, and stock. Cover with aluminum foil and bake at 300° for 3½ hours. The meat should be very tender and falling off the bone. Remove the rabbit with a slotted spoon. Strain the sauce through a fine sieve. Reduce the sauce until it coats the spoon. Season with salt and pepper.

To make the mashed potatoes, in a saucepan, cover the potatoes with cold salted water and simmer for about 30 minutes, until fully cooked. Drain, and peel while hot. In a mixing bowl, mash the potatoes until smooth. In a saucepan over medium heat, cook the garlic and shallots in the butter until soft. Add the cream. Season with salt and pepper.

Peel and roast the pearl onions in a 300° oven for 5 minutes. (If you prepare the mashed potatoes while the rabbit is roasting, you can roast the onions while the oven's still hot.) Peel the baby carrots and cook in salted water for 3 to 4 minutes.

To serve, divide the mashed potatoes over 8 dinner plates. Place the rabbit pieces on top and pour sauce over the rabbit. Garnish with onions and carrots.

Wine notes: From Burgundy, sans doubt. A full-bodied Pommard would be perfect.

Beef Carpaccio and Oysters with Shaved Hearts of Palm and Tomatillo Essence and Bitter Melon Chutney

In New Orleans, beef is often stuffed with oysters and broiled. In my version, both the beef and the oysters are raw, taking their striking flavor profile from the tomatillo essence. A friend from Mauritius, who lives in Louisiana as well, decided to have his wedding at Dominique's and he asked me to prepare Mauritian food for the reception. I included this Bitter Melon Chutney as one of the condiments. I did not know that it is considered bad luck to serve this particular side dish at a wedding. The groom's mother rushed to the kitchen and made me promptly remove it, saving the couple from a bitter marriage. It's still a good side dish for other occasions though.

SERVES 4

2 POUNDS BEEF TENDERLOIN

2 TABLESPOONS OLIVE OIL

1 POUND HEARTS OF PALM

24 OYSTERS, IN SHELL

Tomatillo Essence

10 TOMATILLO PEPPERS, HUSKS ON

1 JALAPEÑO PEPPER, SEEDED AND JUICED

1 TABLESPOON CILANTRO JUICE (JUICER EXTRACTED)

JUICE OF 2 LIMES

SALT AND PEPPER

Bitter Melon Chutney

1 (1 TO 1½ POUNDS) BITTER MELON

1 TABLESPOON SALT

4 CUPS WATER

2 ONIONS, FINELY SLICED

JUICE OF 2 LEMONS

1 TABLESPOON OLIVE OIL

1 JALAPEÑO PEPPER, SEEDED AND CRUSHED

SALT AND PEPPER

(continued)

(Beef Carpaccio continued)

Freeze the beef for 7 to 8 hours; this makes it easier to carve the thin carpaccio slices.

To prepare the essence, grill the peppers over a preheated grill over low heat with the husk on for 10 minutes. Remove the husks and peel the peppers. Place in a blender and purée until smooth. Strain through a fine sieve into a bowl. Add the jalapeño juice, cilantro juice, lime juice, and salt and pepper to taste.

Take the beef from the freezer and slice very thinly into 25 carpaccio slices. Brush the slices with olive oil. Thinly slice the hearts of palm. Remove the oysters from the shells.

To make the chutney, cut the melon in half, remove the seeds, and grate very fine. In a large bowl, add the water and salt. Allow to soak for 1 hour. Strain, wash the melon thoroughly, and drain well, and add to the onions.

In a separate bowl, mix the lemon juice, olive oil, and jalapeño pepper. Pour over the melon and onions. Season to taste.

To serve, place 5 oyster shells on each individual plate. Place hearts of palm in the shells and cover with tomatillo essence. Wrap the beef carpaccio around the oysters. Place the wrapped oysters on top of the hearts of palm and add more tomatillo sauce. The acidity will serve to quickly cook the beef and oysters. Serve immediately with a dollop of chutney on the side.

Wine notes: I recommend a Semillon from Washington state, perhaps the outstanding 1998 Fries Vineyard, from L'École 41.

Island-Rubbed Steak
with Jicama and Grapefruit Slaw

*T*his steak dish carries a touch of Caribbean spice, set off by the cooling sensation of the slaw.

SERVES 8

Island Rub

4 TABLESPOONS ALLSPICE BERRIES

1 SCOTCH BONNET PEPPER, SEEDED (WEAR GLOVES AND HANDLE WITH CARE!)

¼ CUP STEMMED, CHOPPED FRESH CILANTRO

2 CLOVES GARLIC

2 TABLESPOONS CHOPPED THYME

4 BAY LEAVES, STALKS REMOVED, CHOPPED

1½ CUPS CHOPPED GREEN ONION, GREEN AND WHITE PARTS

SALT

FRESHLY GROUND PEPPER

8 (7-OUNCE) FLANK STEAKS

Jicama-Grapefruit Slaw

2 POUNDS JICAMA ROOT, PEELED AND THINLY SLICED

2 GRAPEFRUITS, PEELED, SECTIONED, AND DICED

1 TABLESPOON GINGER JUICE (JUICER EXTRACTED)

1 TABLESPOON FINELY CHOPPED FRESH MINT

1 CUP MICRO CILANTRO

24 PETITE FENNEL

8 BABY RED CARROTS

2 RED CHAYOGA BEETS, PEELED AND SLICED

(continued)

To make the rub, preheat the oven to 300°. Roast the allspice berries in the oven for 7 minutes. With a mortar and pestle, crush the berries into a powder. Add all the remaining ingredients to the powder and crush together thoroughly to make a paste.

Rub the steak with the rub. Refrigerate for 24 hours.

Grill the steak over a preheated grill over medium heat about 8 minutes, until medium-rare.

To make the slaw, combine all the ingredients in a large mixing bowl.

To serve, place the slaw in the middle of the plate. Slice the flank steak about ¼-inch thick and place on top.

Wine notes: A bottle or two of Jamaica's Red Stripe
beer is the best "wine" with this dish.

Sugarcane Brochette of Sweetbreads with Truffle Mashed Potatoes and Wild Mushroom Jus

A lot of people think I created this dish because I live in Louisiana. The state grows sugarcane for miles and miles along the Mississippi River, and there's no doubt its residents have developed quite a sweet tooth to support the economy. But my island of Mauritius grows sugarcane too, and I grew up using cane strips as I do in this dish: as barbecue skewers. I remember wonderful marlin, tuna, and swordfish were skewered on sugarcane and sizzled over an open fire. I've also learned, along the road, that the Vietnamese use sugarcane as a meat tenderizer, making it perfect for this treatment of poached, then crisp-seared sweetbreads.

SERVES 4

Sweetbreads

8 CUPS VEAL STOCK
(PAGE 18)

24 OUNCES VEAL SWEETBREADS, CLEANED

1 30-INCH STALK SUGARCANE

Truffle Mashed Potatoes

10 YUKON GOLD POTATOES

½ CUP HEAVY CREAM

2 TABLESPOONS TRUFFLE BUTTER

1 TABLESPOON TRUFFLE OIL, SUCH AS
URBANI, AVAILABLE AT GOURMET SHOPS

SALT

PEPPER

SHAVED TRUFFLE, FOR GARNISH

(continued)

(Brochette of Sweetbreads continued)

Wild Mushroom Jus

2 CUPS CABERNET SAUVIGNON WINE

½ CUP MOREL MUSHROOMS, SLICED IN HALF

½ CUP MOUSSERON MUSHROOMS

¼ CUP GOLD OYSTER MUSHROOMS

¼ CUP ENOKI MUSHROOMS

¼ CUP CHOCOLATE OYSTER MUSHROOMS

½ CUP PORCINI MUSHROOMS

½ CUP FINELY CHOPPED SHALLOTS

2 TABLESPOONS GRAPESEED OIL

1 TABLESPOON BUTTER

1½ CUPS VEAL STOCK, REDUCED FROM 8 CUPS (PAGE 18)

2 TABLESPOONS TRUFFLE BUTTER

1 CUP RATATOUILLE (PAGE 132)

SHAVED TRUFFLE, FOR GARNISH

To poach the sweetbreads, in a large stock pot, bring the veal stock to a boil over medium heat. Poach the sweetbreads in the stock until medium rare, about 5 minutes. Drain the sweetbreads, reserving the stock.

Place the sweetbreads in a single layer on a parchment-lined sheet and cover with parchment. Place another sheet pan on top and weight to press the sweetbreads. Refrigerate overnight.

In a saucepan over high heat, reduce the stock to 1½ cups, approximately 15 minutes. Once reduced, cool and set aside for the sauce.

To make the jus, reduce the wine to 1½ cups. In a large sauté pan over medium heat, sauté the mushrooms and shallots with the oil and butter for about 10 minutes, until lightly caramelized. Add the wine reduction to deglaze the pan, keeping on the heat for 2 minutes. Add the veal stock reduction and finish with the truffle butter.

To make the mashed potatoes, in a large stock pot over high heat, bring 4 cups of water to a boil. Boil the potatoes, with skin on, until tender, about 20 minutes. Peel while still hot. Place in a large mixing bowl, mash, and process with a mixer until smooth. In a sauté pan over low heat, combine the cream, truffle butter, and truffle oil until melted and hot, about 2 minutes. Combine the cream mixture with the mashed potatoes and season with salt and pepper to taste.

To make the brochettes, cut the sugarcane stalk into 3 6-inch-long sections. Remove the outer skin and split each lengthwise into four skewers. Remove the sweetbreads from the refrigerator and cut them into 12 equal-sized pieces. Skewer each piece with a sugarcane skewer, 3 per person. To serve, place a ring mold on a plate. Scoop 2 tablespoons mashed potatoes, then 1 tablespoon ratatouille, then another 2 tablespoons mashed potatoes, and sprinkle some shaved truffle on top. Make a teepee over this "sandwich" with the brochettes.

In a medium sauté pan over high heat, sear the brochettes on all sides until crispy on the outside and tender inside, about 10 minutes. Set aside.

To serve, place a ring mold on the center of a plate and fill with the mashed potatoes. Lift the ring mold away and stand the brochettes around the potatoes, forming a "teepee." Finish with jus around the outside.

Wine notes: Go with a rich and silky Sociando-Mallet,
any vintage form 1986 to 1990.

DESSERTS

White and Bittersweet
Chocolate Soufflé

At every table, somebody seems to want a soufflé and is willing to order it in advance to get it. This one is less like the usual "eggy" soufflé than it is like a warm, near-liquid chocolate cake. Your guests should love it every bit as much as mine do.

SERVES 6

White Chocolate

½ POUND WHITE CHOCOLATE

½ CUP BUTTER

1½ CUPS SUGAR

½ CUP CORNSTARCH

4 EGGS

4 YOLKS

1 TEASPOON VANILLA EXTRACT

1 TEASPOON ORANGE ZEST

Bittersweet Chocolate

½ POUND BITTERSWEET CHOCOLATE

¾ CUP BUTTER

2 CUPS SUGAR

½ CUP CORNSTARCH

4 EGGS

4 YOLKS

1 TEASPOON RUM

To prepare the white chocolate portion, melt the chocolate and butter in a double boiler over low heat. In a mixing bowl, combine the sugar and cornstarch. Whisk the chocolate mix into the sugar. Slowly stir in the eggs and yolks. Add the vanilla and zest. Refrigerate while the oven preheats.

To prepare the bittersweet chocolate portion, melt the chocolate and butter in a double boiler. In a mixing bowl, combine the sugar and cornstarch. Whisk the chocolate mixture into the sugar. Slowly stir in the eggs and yolks. Add the rum. Refrigerate while the oven preheats.

Preheat the oven to 350°. In 6 individual ceramic soufflé cups, layer the white and bittersweet chocolate mixtures, 2 layers each, starting with the dark chocolate. Bake for 30 minutes. Serve immediately.

Wine notes: I suggest a sparkling red wine from Banfi, something made from the Brocatto grape and ready to match its chilled bubbles and cheery flavors to the warm, molten chocolate of the soufflé.

Caramelized Poached Pear
with Brick Leaves Croustade and Fig-Armagnac Ice Cream

This dessert was inspired by legendary chef Jean-Louis Palladin (except that Jean-Louis used prunes instead of figs in his ice cream). The brick leaves, which are even more airy than phyllo, make an unbelievable mille-feuille. Note: You'll need to start the figs soaking in Armagnac several days in advance.

SERVES 6

Fig-Armagnac Ice Cream

1 CUP MISSION FIGS

½ CUP ARMAGNAC

1 CUP SUGAR

10 EGG YOLKS

2 CUPS WHOLE MILK

1 CUP HALF-AND-HALF

1 TABLESPOON VANILLA EXTRACT

Poached Pear Croustade

1 750-ML BOTTLE WHITE WINE

4 CUPS GRANULATED SUGAR

15 PEARS

1 CUP CLARIFIED BUTTER

18 SHEETS BRICK LEAVES

To prepare the ice cream, soak the figs in Armagnac for 2 days. Purée and set aside.

In a nonreactive mixing bowl, combine the sugar and egg yolks until the sugar is thoroughly dissolved. In a small saucepan, combine the milk and half-and-half. Bring to a boil. Lower the heat and temper the hot cream mixture by slowly adding some of the yolk mixture, about ½ cup at a time, whisking over low heat until the mixture thickens enough to coat the back of a spoon. Strain through a fine sieve and cool over ice. Add the vanilla, fig purée, and Armagnac. Place the mixture in an ice-cream maker and freeze according to the manufacturer's instructions.

To prepare the pears, in a saucepan combine the wine with 3 cups of the sugar and bring to a simmer. Peel the pears and poach them until fully cooked. Lift out the pears with a slotted spoon, cut in halves, and remove the seeds. Thinly slice the pears lengthwise and set slices on a towel. Set aside.

Preheat the oven to 350°. Brush a sheet pan with the butter. Place 2 sheets of brick leaves side by side to cover the pan. Sprinkle with sugar and bake until lightly crisp, 3 to 4 minutes. Remove from the oven and cool to room temperature on a rack. Repeat the process twice more, so you have 6 baked sheets of leaves.

To serve, cut each brick leaf into slices, like pizza. Build a "napoleon" of two leaves, sliced pears, two more leaves, and more sliced pears. End with leaves. Add a scoop of ice cream on top.

Wine notes: Happily, the Armagnac doesn't overpower the Mission figs in the ice cream. I served this dessert at Dominique's second anniversary dinner, pairing it with a 1986 Matanzas Creek botrytised Semillon. It's a marriage to this day.

Peaches and Mandarin Cream
Marzipan Tartlet
with Green Tea Ice Cream

*H*ere's the perfect finale when peaches are fresh and ripe. Be sure to slice them and place them on the tartlet right when you are ready to serve so the juices don't make the crust soggy.

SERVES 10

Green Tea Ice Cream

6 EGG YOLKS

¼ CUP GRANULATED SUGAR

1 CUP HEAVY CREAM

¼ CUP WHOLE MILK

¼ CUP HALF-AND-HALF

1 TEASPOON GREEN TEA POWDER

Mandarin Cream

3 CUPS PASTRY CREAM (PAGE 171)

3 TABLESPOONS MANDARIN ORANGE-FLAVORED VODKA

JUICE OF 1 MANDARIN ORANGE

5 UNPEELED PEACHES, SLICED

Marzipan Tartlet

1 POUND BUTTER

1 POUND SUGAR

½ CUP TOASTED, CHOPPED ALMONDS

2 TABLESPOONS ALMOND EXTRACT

2 EGGS

¼ TEASPOON SALT

1½ CUPS ALL-PURPOSE FLOUR

In a nonreactive mixing bowl, combine the egg yolks and sugar until the sugar is thoroughly dissolved. In a small saucepan, combine the cream, milk, half-and-half, and green tea powder. Bring to a boil. Temper the hot cream mixture by slowly adding some of the yolk mixture, about ½ cup at a time, whisking over low heat until the mixture thickens. Strain through a fine sieve and cool over ice. Transfer the mixture to an ice-cream maker and freeze according to the manufacturer's instructions.

To prepare the marzipan crust, cream the butter, sugar, and almonds together in a mixer. Add the almond extract, eggs, and salt, and mix. Slowly mix in the flour. Form a ball of dough and refrigerate until firm, about 1 hour.

Preheat the oven to 350°. To form the crust, roll the dough out to ¼-inch thickness and mold it into 10 tartlet pans. Bake for 15 minutes.

To prepare the mandarin cream, mix the pastry cream, vodka, and juice together.

To serve, pour the mixture into the tartlet shells. Smooth the top of the cream with a spatula. Fan the sliced peaches on top. Serve with the ice cream on the side.

Wine notes: For an unusual choice, go with a 1992 Royal Tokaji from Hungary. You'll love it. Though this wine, like my beloved Chateau d'Yquem from Sauternes, gets better with age, I choose only those vintages from 1992 and later. That's when the shortcuts taken with the wine under communism were replaced with high wine-making standards.

Banana Rum Fettuccine
with Coconut Crème Anglaise
and Shaved Chocolate Truffle

*H*ere is a dish that is as much fun to look at as it is to eat, and it's sure to bring smiles when you prepare it for friends. The whole thing is a sweet parody of Fettuccine Alfredo—complete with deliciously fake pasta, creamy sauce, and shaved truffles—so when the dish is presented, it looks like a savory main course, but—surprise!—it's a dessert.

SERVES 6

Coconut Crème Anglaise

1 CUP CREAM

1 CUP UNSWEETENED COCONUT MILK

¼ CUP SUGAR

8 EGG YOLKS

1 TEASPOON RUM

Chocolate Truffle

½ CUP HEAVY CREAM

4 OUNCES DARK (SEMISWEET OR BITTERSWEET) CHOCOLATE, CHOPPED

1 TABLESPOON RUM

3 TABLESPOONS COCOA POWDER

Banana Rum Fettuccine

½ POUND ALL-PURPOSE FLOUR

¼ POUND SEMOLINA FLOUR

1 TEASPOON GRAPESEED OIL

¼ CUP BROWN SUGAR

1 RIPE BANANA, PURÉED

4 EGG YOLKS

To prepare the crème anglaise, in a small pot, heat the cream, coconut milk, and sugar to a simmer. In a bowl, mix the egg yolks and rum. Slowly stir the hot coconut cream mixture into the egg-yolk mixture. Refrigerate until chilled.

To make the truffle, in a small pot, heat the cream to a simmer. Remove from the heat and add the chocolate and rum. Refrigerate for 1 hour. When solid, form into a 1½-inch-thick log and roll in cocoa powder. Slice into ¹⁄₁₆ to ⅛-inch slices.

To make the fettuccine, combine the flours, oil, brown sugar, banana, and egg yolks in a mixer until thoroughly blended into a smooth dough. Chill the dough for 30 minutes. With a pasta roller or rolling pin, roll the dough out on a lightly floured board to ¹⁄₁₆-inch thickness. Cut into ¼-inch strips. Cook the fettuccine in boiling water until it floats to the surface. Drain in a colander.

To serve, immediately divide the fettuccine among 6 dinner bowls. Allow the pasta to cool about 3 minutes, then pour ¼ cup of the crème anglaise over each serving. Place truffle slices around the edge of each serving.

Wine notes: To go with the fun, I'd like a sweet Riesling from Germany.

Island Fruit Soup
with Lychee Sorbet

*H*ere's another highly visual dessert: taking the form of a soup, but borrowing the flavors of fruits from the tropics.

SERVES 8

Island Fruit Soup

1 RIPE MANGO

½ CANTALOUPE

1 RIPE PAPAYA

½ CUP CACTUS PEAR PURÉE

1 CUP GUAVA PURÉE

½ CUP PASSION FRUIT PURÉE

¼ CUP GRAND MARNIER

Lychee Sorbet

1 CUP CANE SUGAR

1½ CUPS WARM WATER

2 CUPS LYCHEE PURÉE

2 TABLESPOONS FRESHLY SQUEEZED LEMON JUICE

To prepare the fruit soup, remove all skin and seeds from the fruits. In a blender, finely chop the mango and cantaloupe. Cut the papaya into raisin-sized pieces, mix with the cactus pear purée, and refrigerate. (The papaya–cactus pear mixture will be used to garnish the soup.)

Combine the mango and cantaloupe with the guava and passion fruit purées, and add the Grand Marnier. Chill for 1 hour.

To make the sorbet, combine the sugar and water to form a simple syrup. Add the lychee purée and lemon juice. In an ice-cream maker, freeze until stiff, then place in the freezer for 3 hours.

To serve pour the fruit soup into 8 bowls. Put a 1-ounce scoop of sorbet in each bowl. Put 3 spoonfuls of the papaya/cactus pear mixture on top.

Avocado and Mango Mousse

People who know avocado only in its popular forms, including guacamole, forget that it's actually a fruit. You'll be delighted by the flavor and creaminess avocado brings to this mousse of tropical tastes.

SERVES 8

1 RIPE AVOCADO, PURÉED

1 CUP MANGO PURÉE

1 TEASPOON ALMOND EXTRACT

½ CUP EGG WHITES

1 CUP CANE SUGAR

½ CORN SYRUP

1 CUP HEAVY CREAM

3 TABLESPOONS UNFLAVORED GELATIN

3 TABLESPOONS DARK RUM

MANGO SLICES, FOR GARNISH

½ CUP MACADAMIA NUTS, CHOPPED, FOR GARNISH

Fold the avocado and mango together with the almond extract. Whip the egg whites to stiff peaks. Combine the sugar and corn syrup and heat to 220°. Incorporate into the egg whites and chill. Whip the heavy cream to medium peaks. Combine the gelatin and rum and heat until the gelatin dissolves. Set aside.

Fold half of the egg white meringue and half of the cream into the avocado-mango mixture. Fold in the remaining meringue and cream. Fold in the warm gelatin mixture and refrigerate to set.

To serve, fill a pastry bag and pipe the mixture onto each individual serving plate. Garnish with mango and nuts.

Wine notes: With this dessert, try a Muscat Beaumes de Venice.

Pineapple Confiture

A confiture is like a jam. In Mauritius, every household makes its own confiture to spread on toast, crepes, and sandwiches. At school we would swap sandwiches with one another for the taste of different confitures. I can remember almost all my classmates wanting to swap with me, as my mom made the best pineapple confiture. Other favorites are guava, papaya, and mango. Half-ripe fruit gives a better texture.

MAKES 2 CUPS

2 HALF-RIPE PINEAPPLES

1 CUP PALM SUGAR, OR 2 CUPS
REGULAR SUGAR

1 VANILLA BEAN, SPLIT IN HALF

1 CUP FRESHLY SQUEEZED ORANGE JUICE

1 TEASPOON LEMON ZEST

Peel the pineapples and dice. In a saucepan over medium heat, melt the sugar with the vanilla bean and orange juice. Add the lemon zest. Cook over a low heat for 35 minutes. When done, it should have a jam-like consistency. If stored in a sealed, sterilized jar, it will keep refrigerated for 2 to 3 months.

Guava Ice Cream

With the hot tropical island climate of Mauritius, ice cream is a favorite treat. I prefer to make a Crème Anglaise first and then just have fun with it.

MAKES 1 QUART

1 CUP SUGAR

1½ CUPS WATER

1 VANILLA BEAN, SPLIT IN HALF

2 POUNDS GUAVA, CLEANED AND CUT IN QUARTERS

CRÈME ANGLAISE (PAGE 162, WITHOUT THE COCONUT MILK)

In a pan over medium heat, dissolve the sugar, water, and vanilla. Add the guava and simmer over low heat for 30 minutes. Allow to cool. In a food processor, purée the mixture. Strain through a chinois. Fold in the Crème Anglaise. Freeze in an ice cream maker.

Mango Sorbet

MAKES 1 QUART

1 CUP WATER

1½ CUPS SUGAR

6 MANGOES, PEELED AND SEEDED

In a pan, heat the water and sugar. Allow to cool and add the mango. Purée in a food processor until smooth. In an ice cream maker, freeze until stiff, then place in the freezer for 3 hours before eating.

Crystallized Papaya

*C*rystallized fruit is one of those goodies my grandmother always had tucked away for when she didn't have time to make dessert. It is sweet enough to satisfy the palate after a meal.

MAKES ABOUT 1 POUND

2 PAPAYAS, HALF-RIPE

1 CUP PALM SUGAR

1 CUP FRESHLY SQUEEZED ORANGE JUICE

1 VANILLA BEAN, SPLIT IN HALF

1 TEASPOON LEMON ZEST

Vanilla Sugar

1 CUP SUGAR

1 TEASPOON VANILLA EXTRACT

Peel and seed the papayas. Cut into wedges and set aside.

In a pan over low heat, melt the palm sugar with the orange juice. Add the vanilla bean and zest. Add the papaya wedges and cook over low heat for 15 minutes, until the papaya is soft and has absorbed all the liquid.

To make the vanilla sugar, combine the sugar and the vanilla extract and set aside.

Place the papaya on a sheet pan and place in the sun for 8 to 10 hours. Sprinkle with vanilla sugar every 2 hours. Keep in a closed container for up to 6 months.

Cappamisu
(Jamaican Blue Mountain Tiramisu)

*T*he coffee beans grown on the fertile mountainside of Jamaica's blue mountains are considered the finest in the world. This coffee is also probably the most expensive I have ever come across. But given my own island heritage, I tend to be attracted to all things island-grown, and I don't mind paying the price for quality. I think it makes all the difference in this recipe. I was proud to serve this dessert at the close of my third guest appearance at the James Beard House in New York in August 1999.

SERVES 10

Mocha Wafers

6 EGG YOLKS

½ CUP BREWED BLUE MOUNTAIN COFFEE

½ CUP UNSWEETENED COCOA POWDER

3 TABLESPOONS CORN SYRUP

4 CUPS SUGAR

6 EGG WHITES

1 TEASPOON SALT

4 CUPS ALL-PURPOSE FLOUR

Pastry Cream

1 CUP HEAVY CREAM

1 CUP WHOLE MILK

½ CUP SUGAR

1 TABLESPOON VANILLA

1 TABLESPOON UNFLAVORED GELATIN

2 TABLESPOONS WATER

4 EGG YOLKS

1 CUP CORNSTARCH

Coffee Cream

1 CUP PASTRY CREAM (RECIPE ABOVE)

½ POUND MASCARPONE CHEESE

2 CUPS HEAVY CREAM

½ CUP BREWED BLUE MOUNTAIN COFFEE

1 TABLESPOON KAHLÚA LIQUEUR

1 TABLESPOON BRANDY

1 TEASPOON GROUND ALLSPICE

Kahlúa Coffee

2 OUNCES BREWED BLUE MOUNTAIN COFFEE

1 OUNCE HEAVY CREAM

1 OUNCE KAHLÚA LIQUEUR

10 CAPPUCCINO CHOCOLATE CUPS (PURCHASED)

To make the wafers, preheat the oven to 350°. In a stainless-steel bowl, mix together the egg yolks, coffee, cocoa powder, and corn syrup until smooth. Whip in 2 cups of the sugar. Set aside. In a large stainless-steel bowl, whip together the egg whites and salt until soft peaks form. Add the remaining 2 cups of sugar and whip until stiff peaks form. Fold the egg-yolk mixture into the egg-white mixture. Sift the flour in, one cup at a time, stirring in each addition. Mix the dough until smooth. Drop heaping tablespoons onto a greased baking sheet. Bake for 10 minutes. Cool on a rack.

To make the pastry cream, in a small saucepan, heat the cream, milk, sugar, and vanilla until it comes to a simmer. In a bowl, soften the gelatin with 2 tablespoons of water. Add the egg yolks and cornstarch to the gelatin. Slowly pour the hot cream mixture into the egg mixture, stirring constantly. Refrigerate for 3 hours. Leftover cream keeps up to 3 days in the refrigerator and is great for filling profiterolles or icing cakes.

To make the coffee cream, combine the pastry cream and mascarpone cheese in a mixer. Whip in the heavy cream, coffee, Kahlúa, brandy, and allspice.

To make the coffee, stir all the ingredients together.

To serve, fill a pastry bag with the coffee cream and pipe it into each of 10 glass coffee cups until a third full. Place a mocha wafer on top of the filling. Pour about 1 tablespoon Kahlúa coffee on top of the wafer. Fill the cup to the top with more coffee cream and flatten with a spatula. Refrigerate for 1 hour before serving.

Wine notes: At the Beard House dinner, we enjoyed a pre-release of the 1996 Dolce from California. I'm confident you will enjoy it too.

White Chocolate Bomb
with Coconut Mousse Filling and Mango Coulis

Real coconuts never had it so good! This one, formed of white chocolate, has tropical coconut mousse inside, not to mention a mango surprise.

SERVES 10

Sponge Cake (bottom)

3 EGG YOLKS

1 TABLESPOON VANILLA EXTRACT

1 TABLESPOON FRESHLY SQUEEZED LEMON JUICE

3 EGG WHITES

1 CUP CONFECTIONERS' SUGAR

1½ CUPS CAKE FLOUR

½ CUP FLORENTINE MIX

Mango Coulis (filling and sauce)

1 OR 2 MEDIUM SIZE MANGOES

¼ CUP SUGAR

Mousse

2 CUPS COCONUT MILK

¼ CUP SUGAR

1 TABLESPOON UNFLAVORED GELATIN

1 EGG YOLK

1 CUP WHIPPED CREAM

3 TABLESPOONS MALIBU COCONUT RUM

LEMON JUICE FROM ½ LEMON

Chocolate Cover

6 OUNCES WHITE CHOCOLATE

MANGOES, FOR GARNISH

BERRIES, FOR GARNISH

To prepare the sponge cake, preheat the oven to 430°. Beat the egg yolks, vanilla, and lemon juice until creamy. Set aside. Beat the egg whites and slowly add the confectioners' sugar until creamy. Carefully fold the egg white mixture into the egg yolk mixture. Mix together the flour and florentine mix. Add the egg mixture to the flour mixture. Line a baking sheet pan with parchment paper. Spread the mixture onto the sheet pan. Bake for about 6 minutes until light brown in color. Allow to cool. Cut into 10 rounds to form the bottom of the bomb.

To prepare the mangoes, peel and cut them into small pieces. Add the sugar and purée. Strain through a fine sieve. Divide half of the mixture into 10 small round portions and freeze. The other half will be used as garnish.

To make the mousse, heat the coconut milk with the sugar. Soften the gelatin in cold water for about 5 minutes. Stir the hot coconut milk into the egg yolk in a double boiler. Heat again and continue stirring for about 5 minutes, until the eggs are cooked. Remove from heat. Add the gelatin. Place the mixture in a mixing bowl. Prepare a larger bowl with ice cubes and place the smaller mixing bowl into it. Stir the mixture, keeping it cold at all times. Whip the cream and add carefully to the cold mixture. Add the rum and lemon juice. Refrigerate for 2 hours.

To make the chocolate cover, melt the white chocolate in a bain-marie, or water bath. Form a thin shell of chocolate inside 10 round rubber forms by spreading it carefully around each one. Place in the refrigerator for about 6 minutes.

To serve, remove the chocolate-lined rubber forms from the refrigerator and fill about half full with mousse. Place a layer of frozen mango on top. Add another layer of mousse. Place the sponge cake rounds on top of the layered chocolate/mango forms. Return to the refrigerator for about 5 minutes to hold the form. Remove and invert onto a small plate. Garnish with the mangoes and berries. Pour the mango sauce all around.

Index

A

Ahi tuna
  about, xix
  and crispy pineapple
    mille-feuille, 37–38
Almonds
  peaches and mandarin
    cream marzipan
    tartlet, 160–61
Apples
  and celery root purée,
    142–44
  -merlot reduction, 111–13
Aquavit-citrus–cured salmon,
  94–95
Araujo, 76, 120, 141
Arctic char on celery root and
  lobster mushroom,
  89–91
Artichoke
  barigoule, baby, 68–69
  soup, shrimp, spinach, and,
    55–56
Asparagus
  and grilled scallops, 77–78
  and Manila clam essence,
    90
Avocado and mango
  mousse, 166

B

Bacon, apple-smoked
  Amish chicken "farci" with,
    117–18
  pig trotter on mâche with,
    140–41
  and split pea soup, 52
  vinaigrette, 79–80
Banana rum fettuccine,
  162–63
Bandol, 97
Banfi, 157
Barolo, 144
Basil-mint oil, 34–35
Beans
  cassoulet of seared Hudson
    Valley duck breast on,
    104–5
  conch, lobster, and white
    bean chowder, 58–59
  pickled legumes, 43–44
Beef
  about Kobe, xxii
  carpaccio and oysters,
    147–48
  island-rubbed steak,
    149–50
  noisette of pancetta
    wrapped Kobe, 134–35

  "tartare," ginger-charred
    Kobe, 43–44
Beer, 101, 150
Bell pepper vinaigrette, red,
  77–78
Bethel Heights, 35
Bitter melon chutney, 147–48
Blue marlin, turmeric-
  crusted, 45–46
Boar, wild, double chop of,
  138–39
Bok choy, baby, grilled
  sesame-crusted chicken
  with, 106–7
Bordeaux, 105, 153
Bouillon, gingered fish, 65
Brancott "B," 95
Bread
  brioche, 111–12
  fig and white corn pain
    perdu, 111–12
Brick leaves
  about, xix
  Asian-style barbecue duck
    rillette on, 114–15
  croustade, caramelized
    poached pear with,
    158–59